The Story of Sara

Redefining Leadership Through Service and Vision

Jerry D. Ashley

Disclaimer

This book, The Story of Sarah Mullally, is an independent work of research, interpretation, and commentary. While every effort has been made to ensure accuracy, the author and publisher make no representations or warranties with respect to the completeness, accuracy, or applicability of the contents. The information presented herein is provided for general informational and educational purposes only.

The views, reflections, and interpretations expressed in this book are those of the author and do not necessarily reflect the official views or positions of Sarah Mullally, the Church of England, or any affiliated organizations. Any errors or omissions are unintentional and the sole responsibility of the author.

This book is not authorized, sponsored, endorsed, or otherwise approved by Sarah Mullally or the Church of England. References to individuals, organizations, speeches, or published works are made in good faith for the purposes of commentary, education, and fair use.

Readers are encouraged to consult official sources, primary documents, and verified publications for further information. Neither the author nor the publisher shall be liable for any loss, injury, or damages arising directly or indirectly from the use of this book or reliance on its content.

Table Of Contents

Introduction

Why Sarah Mullally's Story Matters

To understand why the life and leadership of Dame Sarah Mullally matters, one must first look at the crossroads where her journey unfolds: faith and service, compassion and authority, tradition and transformation. In an era where institutions—be they religious, political, or social—struggle to regain the trust of those they claim to serve, Sarah Mullally stands as a rare example of integrity, empathy, and courage in leadership. Her story matters because it embodies the kind of hope that is both urgently needed and deeply resonant in the modern world.

Sarah Mullally's life story is more than a personal biography; it is a reflection of the wider cultural and spiritual shifts that have marked Britain, the Church of England, and indeed global Christianity in the late twentieth and early twenty-first centuries. Born into a society still wrestling with questions of gender roles, professional identity, and religious authority, she became not only a participant in these debates but also a figure who shaped them. She rose to prominence first as a nurse, later as the Chief Nursing Officer for England—the youngest to ever hold the post—and then, through a calling that surprised even herself, as an ordained minister and eventually the Bishop of London.

Each stage of her life underscores an extraordinary commitment to service. Whether at the hospital bedside, the administrative office, or the pulpit of St. Paul's Cathedral, Sarah has insisted that leadership begins with listening and that authority is not about power but about care. Her story matters because it challenges prevailing narratives that leadership must be assertive to the point of aggression, or that faith belongs to the private sphere and not the public conversation. Instead, her life proclaims a different truth: leadership shaped by compassion is not weakness, but strength; faith practiced in the open is not naïveté, but courage.

At a time when many wonder if institutions can still inspire trust, Sarah Mullally's journey demonstrates that credibility is earned not through dominance but through authenticity. Her presence in the Church of England's highest offices stands as a reminder that the arc of history bends toward greater inclusion, even if progress is neither linear nor uncontested. Her life matters because she embodies the possibility of change—change rooted not in slogans or temporary movements, but in steady, faithful service across decades.

The story of Sarah Mullally also matters for another reason: it is deeply human. Behind the robes of episcopal office, beyond the headlines about "first woman Bishop of London," lies the story of a daughter, a wife, a mother, a colleague, and a servant of God. She has wrestled with doubts, navigated moments of tension, and faced the challenge of balancing a demanding public life with the intimacy of private faith. This humanity is precisely what makes her story compelling. For readers of this book—

whether they approach it from the perspective of faith, leadership, gender studies, or personal inspiration—her life offers lessons not in abstract ideals, but in lived experience.

Her story matters, finally, because it is still being written. This book does not close the chapter on Sarah Mullally's legacy; it invites readers into an unfolding narrative, one that will continue to shape lives and communities in ways both visible and hidden for years to come. By studying her journey, we learn not only about her but also about ourselves—our hopes for leaders who heal, our need for institutions that serve, and our longing for faith that speaks to the present age.

The Making of a Modern Faith Leader

To appreciate the full significance of Sarah Mullally's leadership, it is essential to trace the making of her character and the journey that brought her to prominence. Unlike many religious figures whose paths to ministry follow predictable lines of theological training and parish service, Sarah's early career placed her at the intersection of healthcare and leadership long before she ever stepped into a pulpit.

Her background in nursing was not incidental to her later ministry; it was formative. Nursing is a vocation that demands both technical expertise and profound empathy. A nurse must attend to details—the correct dosage of medication, the precise timing of interventions—while simultaneously caring for the whole person: body, mind, and spirit. Sarah thrived in this environment, rising rapidly through the profession. Her appointment as Chief Nursing Officer for England at the age of thirty-eight marked her as one of the youngest leaders in the National Health Service and cemented her reputation as someone who combined competence with compassion.

It is in this period that one begins to see the hallmarks of her later ecclesiastical leadership: attentiveness to the vulnerable, commitment to evidence-based decision-making, and the ability to navigate complex systems with both pragmatism and vision. The making of Sarah Mullally as a modern faith leader did not begin in theological colleges but in hospital wards, where human fragility and resilience are most visible.

Her transition from healthcare to ordained ministry was neither abrupt nor accidental. It emerged from a deepening sense of vocation, a recognition that the call to heal extends beyond the physical and into the spiritual. For Sarah, nursing and priesthood were not competing callings but complementary expressions of the same desire: to care for people in their most vulnerable moments. This integration of professional experience and spiritual calling would become one of the most distinctive features of her ministry.

As she rose through the ranks of the Church of England, Sarah carried with her not only the credibility of her past achievements but also the perspective of someone who had lived and led outside the cloistered world of ecclesiastical hierarchy. She understood institutions because she had worked in them; she valued expertise because she had relied on it; she respected diversity because she had seen it in the NHS workforce and patient population. In short, she brought to the church the mindset of a modern leader—open to dialogue, grounded in service, and unwilling to separate faith from the realities of everyday life.

In the making of Sarah Mullally, one sees the making of a leader uniquely suited to the twenty-first century. She is not a throwback to past forms of religious authority, nor a leader shaped only by internal church debates. Instead, she embodies the integration of secular and sacred, personal and institutional, local and global. This synthesis explains why her appointment as Bishop of London in 2018 was more than a personal milestone; it was a symbolic moment for the entire Church of England, signaling a new era in which the boundaries between service, leadership, and faith could be redrawn in transformative ways.

Themes and Purpose of This Book

This book has been written with one clear purpose: to tell the story of Sarah Mullally in a way that is honest, comprehensive, and meaningful, offering readers not only information but also inspiration. At its core, this is a biography, but it is also more than that—it is a guide to understanding how leadership rooted in compassion can shape institutions, communities, and individuals alike.

Several themes run through the chapters that follow:

1. Leadership as Service
One of the most striking aspects of Sarah Mullally's career is her consistent view that leadership is not about exerting control but about enabling others. Whether in healthcare administration or church leadership, she has insisted that the measure of success lies in the well-being of those she serves. This book will explore how she has redefined leadership for a generation skeptical of authority.

2. Faith in the Public Square
Another key theme is the integration of personal faith with public responsibility. Sarah has never confined her Christianity to private devotion; she has brought it into national conversations about health, ethics, diversity, and social justice. Her life raises vital questions about what it means for faith to shape public life in a pluralistic society.

3. Gender and Inclusion
Sarah Mullally's story cannot be told without reference to the broader struggles for gender equality within the Church of England. Her rise to the episcopacy was not merely a personal triumph but also a collective milestone for women who had long been excluded from positions of senior leadership. This book will examine both the significance and the challenges of that breakthrough.

4. Resilience and Humanity

Behind the public figure lies a human being who has faced challenges, wrestled with doubts, and sought balance between personal and professional life. This theme will remind readers that leadership is not about perfection but about perseverance and authenticity.

5. Legacy in the Making

Finally, this book will trace not only what Sarah has achieved but also what she continues to represent. Her legacy is still unfolding, but the outlines are already visible: a church more inclusive, a model of leadership more compassionate, and a public faith more engaged with the real issues of society.

The purpose of this book is not to idolize or to criticize, but to understand. By telling Sarah Mullally's story in full detail—her background, her achievements, her struggles, her vision—this book seeks to offer readers both knowledge and inspiration. It invites reflection on how one person's journey can illuminate larger questions of faith, leadership, and society.

How to Read This Companion

This book has been structured to serve multiple audiences. Some readers may approach it as a biography, eager to trace the story of Sarah Mullally's life from childhood to her current role as Bishop of London. Others may come to it with an interest in leadership, looking for insights into how a woman navigated the challenges of leading in both healthcare and the church. Still others may be drawn by questions of faith, curious about how Christianity can speak to modern issues of justice, inclusion, and community.

For this reason, the chapters have been arranged chronologically but with thematic depth, allowing readers to either follow the story from beginning to end or to dip into specific sections that align with their interests. The early chapters focus on her background and nursing career, setting the stage for her later ministry. The middle chapters explore her rise through the Church of England, culminating in her historic appointment as Bishop of London. The later chapters examine her theological vision, her handling of controversies, her personal life, and her legacy in progress.

Each chapter seeks not merely to present facts but to engage the reader emotionally and intellectually. Quotations from speeches, reflections from colleagues, and analysis of her decisions will help bring the narrative to life. At the same time, the writing aims to be accessible, avoiding jargon and focusing on clear storytelling.

Readers are encouraged to approach this book not as passive consumers of information but as active participants in reflection. Sarah Mullally's life raises questions that each of us must answer: What does it mean to serve others? How should faith shape our engagement with society? What kind of leadership do we value and why?

This companion is not only the story of one woman but also an invitation to consider our own stories, our own vocations, and our own contributions to the communities we belong to. By reading deeply, thoughtfully, and reflectively, readers will find themselves not only informed about Sarah Mullally but also inspired to think differently about their own paths.

Chapter 1

Early Life and Formative Years

1.1 Childhood and Family Background

When we look at the life of Sarah Mullally, it is tempting to begin at the moment she stepped into the global spotlight as the Bishop of London — a historic appointment that reverberated through the Church of England and beyond. Yet to understand the depth of her character, the values that shaped her, and the steady resilience that carried her through the complexities of leadership, one must begin long before the vestments and the cathedral. Her story, like that of many who rise to lead, is rooted in the everyday details of family life, community, and the quiet but persistent shaping forces of childhood.

Sarah Elisabeth Mullally was born on 26 March 1962, a child of post-war Britain — a Britain that was still rebuilding itself from the scars of conflict, but also entering a period of cultural and social transformation. The early 1960s were years of transition: the decline of the old order of deference, the rise of a new youth culture, and a country beginning to renegotiate its identity in a changing world. Into this environment came Sarah, whose upbringing was not characterized by privilege or excess but by a steady grounding in family values, modest means, and an ethic of service.

Her parents were not figures of great public renown, but they were figures of deep personal influence. Family life provided Sarah with a sense of belonging, structure, and stability. While Britain in the 1960s was wrestling with questions of class, gender, and authority, in her own home she was learning the quieter lessons of kindness, duty, and perseverance. Her parents instilled in her the idea that what mattered most was not status or wealth but the impact one had on the lives of others.

These early family values would later echo in her dual careers — first in nursing, where the measure of success is the healing touch extended to the vulnerable, and then in ministry, where leadership is rooted not in command but in compassion. Childhood, in Sarah's case, was not a prelude to ambition but a seedbed of service.

From accounts of her later reflections, it is clear that her home life was a place where faith and community were interwoven. Christianity was not, in her formative years, merely an abstract belief or a Sunday ritual but part of the rhythm of family life. This early exposure to the rituals of the Church, the moral narratives of Scripture, and the lived example of ordinary people practicing their faith quietly but consistently became the foundation upon which her vocation would one day stand.

It is also important to recognize that her childhood coincided with a period when women's roles in both society and the Church were being debated and redefined. In 1962, the idea of a woman becoming a bishop in the Church of England would have seemed almost impossible. Yet Sarah's childhood taught her not to see barriers as fixed walls but as challenges to be approached with patience, integrity, and courage. Her family's encouragement and the supportive environment they cultivated ensured that she did not grow up constrained by narrow expectations of what a woman could or could not do.

1.2 Education and Early Influences

If home provided the soil, education was the sunlight and water that allowed Sarah's gifts to grow. Her schooling years were critical in shaping not only her intellectual abilities but also her sense of discipline, her confidence, and her developing view of the world.

From an early age, she showed an aptitude for learning. Teachers recognized in her a seriousness of purpose — not the seriousness that isolates, but the kind that quietly inspires others. She was not content merely to memorize facts or pass examinations; she wanted to understand, to make sense of things, and to see how knowledge could be applied in practical, meaningful ways.

Education in Britain of the 1960s and 70s was undergoing shifts. The rise of comprehensive schools was changing the old grammar school system, and universities were opening their doors to broader demographics. For Sarah, this environment offered possibilities, but it also demanded determination. A young woman who wanted to excel had to navigate not only the standard academic pressures but also the lingering cultural biases that questioned whether girls could or should pursue professional careers in fields like science, medicine, or leadership.

One of the formative aspects of Sarah's educational journey was her growing awareness of healthcare and the human body. This interest was not abstract curiosity; it was motivated by a desire to serve. Even as a student, she was fascinated by the intersection of knowledge and compassion — how scientific skill, when guided by empathy, could change lives. This dual interest — the technical and the humane — became the foundation of her career in nursing and later her approach to ministry, where both intellect and empathy are indispensable.

Her teachers and mentors played an important role in encouraging her. There were those who saw her potential and pushed her to reach further than she might have imagined for herself. Their encouragement gave her confidence at a time when young women were often subtly or overtly discouraged from aiming too high. These influences reinforced in her the idea that leadership is not about self-advancement but about using one's gifts for the benefit of others.

But perhaps the most enduring educational influence was not simply academic knowledge but the cultivation of values: resilience, curiosity, and a willingness to listen. These qualities, honed in the classroom and beyond, prepared her for the challenges of both healthcare leadership and spiritual guidance.

1.3 Discovering Her Vocation for Service

The idea of vocation is central to Sarah Mullally's story. Unlike a career, which can be chosen, changed, or abandoned, a vocation is experienced as a calling — something that grips the heart and demands a response. For Sarah, this sense of vocation first revealed itself in healthcare.

From her teenage years, she felt drawn toward nursing. At a time when nursing was often undervalued compared to the prestige of doctors, Sarah saw in it not a secondary role but a profound vocation of care, presence, and dignity. She entered nursing not as a stepping-stone but as a calling in itself.

Her journey into the profession was marked by both skill and determination. She trained rigorously, absorbing not only the clinical skills required but also the deeper ethos of nursing: to treat patients not as cases but as human beings. She quickly distinguished herself as someone who combined technical competence with genuine empathy.

But what is most significant is how she understood this vocation. For Sarah, nursing was never only about the hospital ward or the medical chart. It was about serving the whole person — body, mind, and spirit. This integrated view of care reflected the Christian ethos she had absorbed as a child and reinforced in her educational years.

Yet as the years unfolded, another layer of vocation began to emerge: the call to ministry. At first, she resisted the thought. After all, she was deeply committed to her healthcare career, rising to the position of Chief Nursing Officer for England by the age of 37 — an extraordinary achievement that made her one of the most senior figures in the NHS. But even amid such success, she felt the quiet tug of another calling, one that asked her to bring her gifts of leadership, compassion, and resilience into a different sphere: the Church.

This sense of dual vocation — first in nursing, then in ministry — is one of the most distinctive aspects of Sarah's life. It demonstrates that vocation is not static but dynamic, that God's call can evolve and deepen over time, and that one's early sense of purpose can prepare the ground for later, unexpected callings.

1.4 Values Shaped by Home, Community, and Faith

To fully understand Sarah Mullally's early years, it is essential to look beyond biography to the values that were quietly but powerfully shaping her. These values were not abstract principles but lived realities, formed through her experiences of family, education, community, and early professional service.

Faith was the bedrock. Though she would later articulate her theology in nuanced and sophisticated ways, its roots were in the simple practices of childhood faith: going to church, hearing the stories of Scripture, witnessing acts of kindness and service in the community. These experiences taught her that faith was not primarily about dogma but about living differently in the world — with compassion, humility, and integrity.

Community was another formative influence. Growing up, Sarah learned that individuals are never isolated but always part of a wider web of relationships. This awareness would later define her approach both to healthcare (where the patient is part of a family and community) and to ministry (where the church is a body of interconnected people, not a collection of isolated souls).

Service was perhaps the most distinctive value. From her earliest years, Sarah internalized the idea that life is not about self-promotion but about making a difference. Whether in the ward as a nurse, at the helm of healthcare policy, or in the pulpit as a bishop, her guiding principle has been the same: to serve others with integrity and compassion.

Resilience and courage also emerged early. Growing up as a woman in a world that often limited women's opportunities, Sarah learned to persist without bitterness and to lead without arrogance. These values enabled her to navigate the challenges of senior roles in both the NHS and the Church, where scrutiny, criticism, and controversy are part of the terrain.

By the time she reached adulthood, Sarah Mullally was not only a highly capable young woman with clear professional ambitions; she was also a person deeply shaped by values that would define her entire career. The interplay of faith, family, education, and vocation had forged in her a sense of purpose that was both personal and communal, both practical and spiritual.

Chapter 2

Nursing Career

Before Sarah Mullally was consecrated as one of the most influential leaders in the Church of England, she had already carved out a remarkable career in healthcare. To understand her as a bishop, a visionary, and a pastoral figure, one must first understand her decades of work as a nurse, a profession rooted in compassion, service, and a relentless pursuit of healing. Her journey through the world of nursing was not only about medical skill but also about cultivating the leadership qualities that would later define her episcopal ministry. Nursing taught her the complexities of human suffering, the responsibility of stewardship, and the delicate art of balancing science with empathy.

This chapter explores her entry into nursing, her rapid rise through the profession, her landmark appointment as England's Chief Nursing Officer, and the core principles she carried from the wards of hospitals into the corridors of ecclesiastical power.

2.1 Entering the World of Nursing

Sarah Mullally's decision to pursue nursing was not an arbitrary career choice; it was a vocation in its own right.

Growing up in Britain in the 1960s and 1970s, she was part of a generation witnessing the ongoing evolution of the National Health Service (NHS), a system that symbolized both the promise of universal healthcare and the immense challenges of sustaining it. For many young women at the time, nursing was seen as a respectable profession, one that blended intellectual skill with a moral imperative to serve others.

From an early age, Mullally showed a natural attentiveness to people's needs. Teachers, friends, and family often noted her quiet but determined presence. She possessed both curiosity and compassion — qualities that would define her career. Nursing appealed to her because it was a profession that fused care with responsibility. It was not simply about following medical routines but about entering into the vulnerabilities of people's lives at their most fragile moments.

Choosing nursing also meant stepping into a demanding and often undervalued field. At the time, nursing was undergoing shifts in professional identity, with calls for higher education, expanded roles, and greater recognition. Mullally's decision to enter this world reflected both courage and foresight. She was not content to remain passive; she wanted to actively participate in shaping healthcare.

When she began her training, she quickly discovered that nursing required far more than technical skill. It was an immersive education in human dignity. Days were spent learning anatomy, physiology, pharmacology, and clinical procedures. Nights were often spent comforting anxious patients, listening to fears, or holding a hand in silence. In these formative years, she came to understand that healing was not merely about curing diseases but about affirming humanity in moments of suffering.

2.2 Rising Through the Ranks of Healthcare

From her earliest days on the wards, Mullally distinguished herself with both competence and vision. She was not content to simply execute instructions; she was always asking deeper questions: How can care be improved? How can systems be made more responsive to patients? What could be done to prevent suffering before it escalated?

Her professional progression was marked by a combination of intellectual capacity and emotional intelligence. She rapidly gained the respect of her colleagues not only for her clinical expertise but also for her ability to inspire and organize teams. In the hierarchical world of hospitals, where doctors often overshadowed nurses, Mullally demonstrated the authority of nursing leadership. She understood that nurses were not simply assistants to physicians but crucial agents of patient care, often spending more time with patients than anyone else.

Her career trajectory was anything but ordinary. While many nurses remained within the confines of ward-based care, Mullally quickly advanced into management and policy. Her appointments reflected her ability to blend frontline experience with strategic oversight. She took on roles that demanded broader vision: overseeing staff, shaping policy, and innovating systems of care.

By the 1990s, the NHS faced significant strain. Resources were stretched, patient demand was rising, and healthcare workers often bore the brunt of systemic inefficiencies. Mullally was at the forefront of confronting these challenges, advocating for reforms that prioritized both patient safety and the well-being of healthcare workers. Her leadership style was characterized by pragmatism grounded in empathy. She believed that sustainable healthcare required not only financial efficiency but also moral responsibility.

2.3 Becoming England's Chief Nursing Officer

In 1999, Sarah Mullally achieved what many would later describe as the pinnacle of her healthcare career: she was appointed Chief Nursing Officer (CNO) for England, the most senior nursing position in the nation. At the age of just 41, she became one of the youngest people ever to hold the role. Her appointment was not only a personal milestone but also a symbolic moment for the profession.

As CNO, she was responsible for overseeing the direction of nursing policy across the entire NHS. The role demanded vision, resilience, and the ability to navigate political pressures. At the turn of the millennium, the NHS was undergoing transformation, with new technologies, expanding patient expectations, and constant debates about funding. Nurses were increasingly being recognized as leaders in their own right, yet the profession still struggled for full acknowledgment in the public sphere.

Mullally's tenure as CNO was marked by her insistence that nursing should be seen not just as a caring role but as a profession of high expertise, leadership, and innovation. She worked tirelessly to strengthen professional standards, improve patient safety protocols, and elevate the visibility of nursing as a cornerstone of healthcare.

One of her defining priorities was workforce development. She championed initiatives to recruit, train, and retain nurses at a time when staffing shortages were a growing concern. She recognized that a resilient NHS depended not just on policies written in offices but on the dedication of thousands of nurses on the ground. To that end, she emphasized mentorship, continuing education, and leadership opportunities within nursing.

Mullally also worked to bridge the gap between policymakers and practitioners. She believed that effective healthcare reform required listening to those delivering care at the bedside. Her approach combined the authority of her office with the humility of a nurse who had once changed bandages, administered medication, and comforted patients in the quiet hours of the night.

Her leadership as CNO was not without its challenges. She had to confront difficult issues such as resource allocation, the rising complexity of healthcare needs, and debates over modernization. Yet through it all, she remained a steady advocate for patient-centered care. Her reputation grew not only within healthcare but also across government and the public. By the time she stepped away from the post in 2004, she had cemented her legacy as one of the most influential nurse leaders in modern British history.

2.4 Compassion, Care, and Leadership in Action

What set Mullally apart in her nursing career was not only her ability to lead but also her capacity to embody compassion at scale. Compassion was not for her a soft or secondary quality; it was the foundation of effective healthcare. To lead without compassion, she believed, was to risk turning medicine into bureaucracy rather than healing.

Her colleagues often remarked on her ability to connect with people at every level. Whether speaking with government officials, addressing professional conferences, or visiting hospital wards, she carried herself with attentiveness and humility. Her leadership was not imposed from above but drawn from within a community of shared values. She understood that true authority was not about commanding compliance but about inspiring trust.

In her speeches and interviews, Mullally frequently emphasized the ethical dimensions of healthcare. She argued that patients should not be reduced to case numbers or diagnoses but seen as whole persons with fears, hopes, and stories. This holistic perspective reflected her conviction that healing was as much about dignity as it was about cure.

Her approach also extended to how she treated her colleagues. She consistently advocated for nurses to be respected, supported, and given opportunities to flourish. She recognized the emotional toll of the profession and encouraged systems that acknowledged the humanity of healthcare workers themselves. To care for the carer, she argued, was essential if patients were to receive the best possible treatment.

These values of compassion and care would later resonate deeply in her ecclesiastical career. Many observed that her pastoral style as a bishop bore the imprint of her years in nursing: listening attentively, responding practically, and leading with a balance of authority and gentleness.

2.5 Lessons from the Frontlines of Health

Looking back, Mullally has often acknowledged that her years in nursing were formative in shaping her as a leader and as a Christian. The hospital ward became, in many ways, her first pulpit. The lessons she carried from healthcare into ministry were profound and lasting.

First, she learned the discipline of presence. Nursing requires attentiveness to the moment: being fully present with a patient in crisis, even when schedules are crowded and pressures immense. This capacity for presence became central to her pastoral care, reminding her that leadership is not just about vision but about showing up for people in their need.

Second, she internalized the importance of teamwork. No single nurse, doctor, or administrator can sustain a healthcare system alone. Success depends on collaboration, respect, and shared responsibility. Later, as Bishop of London, she would apply this same principle to church leadership, seeing herself not as a solitary authority but as part of a wider body working together for the good of communities.

Third, she experienced the limits of human effort. In healthcare, not every patient can be saved, not every illness can be cured. These moments of loss taught her humility and resilience. They also deepened her theological understanding of suffering and mortality, insights that would later shape her preaching and pastoral presence.

Finally, nursing instilled in her a relentless commitment to justice. She saw firsthand how poverty, inequality, and systemic failures could compound illness. These experiences seeded a conviction that faith and leadership must confront social as well as personal issues. Her advocacy for inclusion, equality, and dignity within the Church of England can be traced directly to the justice she pursued in healthcare.

By the time Sarah Mullally left her position as Chief Nursing Officer in 2004, she was already preparing to enter ordained ministry. Yet her story as a nurse was not an isolated chapter but a foundation for all that would follow. She carried from the wards of hospitals into the pulpits of cathedrals a vision of leadership that was grounded in compassion, justice, and service.

Her nursing career remains a testament to the power of healing hands guided by a discerning mind and a compassionate heart. It revealed a leader who understood that service is the highest form of authority and that to heal is to affirm the dignity of every human life. These lessons would echo profoundly in her journey through the Church, making her one of the most distinctive and influential bishops of her generation.

Chapter 3

Answering the Call to Ministry

For much of Sarah Mullally's life, vocation was not a single, static word but a living, breathing journey. To the outside world, she had already achieved more than most could dream of. Rising from a determined nurse to England's Chief Nursing Officer, she stood as one of the most respected leaders in healthcare. Yet, beneath the layers of professional achievement lay a quieter, deeper stirring—one that no job title, however prestigious, could satisfy. It was a calling to ministry, a vocation that demanded courage, humility, and a profound reordering of life itself.

This chapter explores that pivotal transition: how a woman at the peak of one career embraced the vulnerability of beginning another; how she entered the rigorous, often daunting process of ordination; how she juggled family, personal faith, and professional expectations; and how, through persistence and grace, she helped break boundaries for women in the Church of England. Sarah Mullally's journey from nurse to bishop was not a straight path, nor was it devoid of challenge. But in the complexity of this calling, we see the depth of her faith and the strength of her character.

3.1 Transition from Nursing to Theology

By the late 1990s, Sarah Mullally had already earned distinction as one of Britain's leading healthcare professionals. At the age of thirty-eight, she had become England's youngest Chief Nursing Officer—a position that put her at the very center of national health policy. She was advising ministers, shaping healthcare strategy, and representing thousands of nurses and midwives. To many, this was the pinnacle of a career. For Sarah, however, it was not the destination.

Throughout her years in healthcare, Sarah had always nurtured a sense of faith. Raised within the rhythms of the Church of England, her spirituality was not a sideline to her professional duties but an undercurrent, infusing her approach to leadership and compassion. Patients were never simply "cases" or "statistics" to her; they were individuals, each carrying a sacred worth. This deep sense of dignity and calling resonated with her faith and began to tug her toward ministry.

The decision to step away from healthcare was not sudden. It emerged through years of discernment, prayer, and listening. For Sarah, vocation was not about abandoning her achievements but about following a deeper voice. As she later described, nursing had been a calling in itself, a way of healing and serving. Yet the transition to theology was about broadening that service, moving from the hospital ward to the parish, from the policies of health to the pastoral care of souls.

The moment of decision was layered with complexity. There was the fear of leaving behind a secure and respected position. There were questions from colleagues and friends—why give up such influence, such visibility? Yet Sarah recognized that her success in nursing, while fulfilling, did not quiet the deeper sense of being drawn to ministry. It was a leap of faith, one that required courage to leave the known for the unknown.

Her story in this period resonates with countless individuals who feel torn between worldly success and spiritual calling. But unlike many, Sarah chose the riskier road, trusting that the skills she had honed in healthcare—leadership, empathy, resilience—would translate into the ministry of the Church. This was not about abandoning her past, but about carrying it into a new vocation where the gifts of healing and leadership could serve in new ways.

3.2 Training for Ordination

Entering the path toward ordination was both exhilarating and daunting. The Church of England's process of discernment is deliberately rigorous, designed to test whether a candidate's calling is authentic, sustainable, and suited to the demands of ministry. For Sarah, this was a period of both self-examination and growth.

Her theological training took place at the South East Institute for Theological Education, a part-time program that allowed her to continue balancing professional commitments while immersing herself in study. This dual approach was well suited to someone like Sarah, whose life had long been marked by balancing multiple responsibilities.

Theology opened new horizons for her. She delved into scripture with fresh eyes, learning not just to read but to interpret, to situate the biblical narrative within history and to ask what it demanded of the Church today. Courses in pastoral theology resonated deeply with her nursing background, offering frameworks for care that extended beyond the physical to the spiritual and emotional. She engaged with liturgy, church history, ethics, and doctrine, developing a toolkit that would equip her for parish ministry.

Yet training was not merely academic. It was also spiritual and personal. Candidates were expected to examine their own lives, to consider how they embodied the values of the Gospel, and to recognize their own limitations. For someone with Sarah's accomplished background, humility was key. She had been a national leader, yet now she was once again a student, learning alongside others, submitting to formation rather than authority.

The ordination process also required formal assessments, interviews, and spiritual direction. Bishops and selectors evaluated her capacity for leadership, her resilience under pressure, her ability to communicate faith authentically, and her readiness to embrace the sacrificial aspects of ministry. Sarah's previous career gave her an unusual strength: she had already navigated crises, managed large teams, and led with integrity. These qualities, combined with her deepening faith, made her a compelling candidate.

In 2001, Sarah Mullally was ordained as a deacon, and a year later, as a priest in the Church of England. These milestones marked not just the culmination of training but the beginning of a new life. The ordination ceremony itself was profoundly symbolic. To kneel, receive prayer and blessing, and rise as a minister of the Church was an act of surrender, a declaration that her life's direction now belonged wholly to God.

3.3 Balancing Family, Faith, and Professional Life

The call to the ministry was not answered in isolation. Like many clergy, Sarah had to navigate the complexities of family life alongside her professional responsibilities and spiritual commitments. This balancing act became one of the defining features of her early ministry.

Sarah is married to Eamonn Mullally, and together they have children. The shift into ministry inevitably reshaped family rhythms. Parish life often demanded evenings, weekends, and pastoral emergencies at unexpected hours. For a family already accustomed to the demands of healthcare, the transition still brought new challenges. The parsonage, unlike an office, is not a private retreat but an extension of ministry, with parishioners frequently crossing its threshold.

Balancing these demands required intentional boundaries, open communication, and mutual support. Sarah often emphasized that ministry was not hers alone but something in which her family participated. Whether attending services, hosting parish events, or simply being present in the community, the Mullally family lived within the reality that ministry is both personal and communal.

Faith was the anchor that made this balance possible. Prayer and reflection were not optional extras but lifelines. Sarah has spoken of the importance of daily rhythms of prayer, scripture, and silence as a way of grounding herself amidst the busyness of ministry. These practices not only sustained her but also modeled for her family what it meant to live with faith at the center.

Her background in nursing also played a role. Having managed high-pressure roles before, she understood the importance of prioritization and resilience. She brought the same discipline and clarity to ministry: focusing on what mattered most, delegating where necessary, and learning to say no when boundaries were at risk.

Balancing faith, family, and ministry is a struggle shared by many clergy, and Sarah's example demonstrates that it is possible not through perfection but through honesty, support, and reliance on grace.

3.4 Breaking Boundaries as a Woman in the Church

Perhaps the most historically significant aspect of Sarah Mullally's call to ministry was the fact that she was a woman entering a church still wrestling with questions of gender and leadership. While the ordination of women had been approved by the Church of England in 1992, and women had begun serving as priests from 1994, the full acceptance of women in positions of leadership remained contested well into the 2000s.

For Sarah, entering ministry was therefore both personal and political. On one hand, it was simply obedience to God's call. On the other, it placed her at the forefront of a wider movement for equality and recognition within the church. As a woman, she would face scrutiny, skepticism, and at times outright opposition. Yet her background gave her a resilience that proved invaluable.

In healthcare, Sarah had already navigated leadership in a field where women were often underrepresented in senior positions. She knew what it meant to lead with authority while facing gendered assumptions. In ministry, these skills translated into quiet confidence and determination. She did not seek to prove herself through confrontation but through consistent, faithful service.

Her ordination was also symbolic for many women in the church. It demonstrated that leadership in ministry was not confined to men, that women's gifts were equally valid, and that the church could be enriched by their perspectives. Sarah's presence challenged stereotypes not by words alone but by example: a leader who combined competence with compassion, intellect with humility.

Over time, her leadership helped pave the way for other women in the Church of England. She became part of a generation that normalized the presence of female clergy, making it increasingly difficult for opponents to argue that women lacked the capacity or calling for such roles. Her later rise to bishop would make history, but its roots lay in these early years, when she chose to step forward despite resistance.

The Courage to Begin Again

Sarah Mullally's call to ministry is a story of courage, discernment, and transformation. It is the story of a woman willing to leave behind the security of one career to embrace the uncertainty of another, trusting that the God who called her would equip her. It is the story of a leader who recognized that vocation is not about status but about service, not about ambition but about obedience.

In making the transition from nursing to theology, she demonstrated that faith can reorient even the most successful life. In training for ordination, she submitted herself to learning and formation, embracing humility and growth. In balancing family, faith, and ministry, she modeled integrity and resilience. And in breaking boundaries as a woman in the church, she became a pioneer, opening doors for others and reshaping what leadership looks like in the body of Christ.

This chapter of her life reminds us that vocation is rarely linear. It is often a journey marked by detours, doubts, and decisions that require courage. Yet for Sarah Mullally, answering the call to ministry was not just a career change—it was the defining step that would shape her legacy as one of the most influential leaders of faith in contemporary Britain.

Chapter 4

Serving the Church of England

The story of Sarah Mullally's service in the Church of England is as much a personal pilgrimage of faith as it is a reflection of the institution's own evolving identity. To understand her impact, one must first appreciate the context in which she entered ministry. The Church of England in the late 20th and early 21st centuries was wrestling with deep questions of relevance, inclusivity, and identity. Against this backdrop, Mullally's decision to leave behind one of the most senior roles in the National Health Service and embrace the uncertainties of parish ministry was not merely a personal career change — it was a profound act of faith, service, and obedience.

Her journey through parish ministry, pastoral work, and community leadership highlights a remarkable capacity to listen, adapt, and lead. It also reflects her unique combination of professional competence, spiritual depth, and practical compassion — qualities that would later distinguish her in the upper echelons of the Church.

4.1 Early Roles in Parish Ministry

When Sarah Mullally entered parish ministry, she was not simply stepping into a new job — she was immersing herself in a centuries-old tradition of service, worship, and pastoral responsibility. For someone who had already risen to the highest professional levels of nursing, parish life presented an entirely different set of demands. Instead of the systems and hierarchies of healthcare administration, she now found herself navigating the intimate, relational, and often unpredictable realities of parish communities.

Her first parish assignments were both a testing ground and a classroom. She learned quickly that parish ministry demanded more than theological knowledge or liturgical precision. It required the ability to inhabit the daily lives of ordinary people, to share in their joys and sorrows, and to become a trusted presence in moments of vulnerability. Weddings, baptisms, and funerals placed her at the center of people's most sacred milestones, while pastoral visits to homes, schools, and hospitals required her to embody Christ's compassion in practical and tangible ways.

These early years revealed her natural gifts for listening and empathy. Parishioners frequently remarked on her capacity to make them feel heard and valued. Unlike some clergy who approached ministry from a position of authority, Mullally's approach was shaped by her nursing background: attentive, non-judgmental, and always rooted in a deep respect for the dignity of each person. Her leadership was not about control, but about accompaniment.

At the same time, she encountered the challenges familiar to any new priest. She had to balance the administrative responsibilities of parish life — managing budgets, overseeing volunteers, maintaining church buildings — with the spiritual demands of preaching, teaching, and pastoral care. These competing priorities tested her ability to remain centered, to find time for prayer and reflection amidst the relentless demands of parish life. Yet, far from being overwhelmed, Mullally thrived. She treated each challenge as an opportunity to grow, to deepen her trust in God, and to refine her sense of vocation.

It was also during these years that she began to develop a reputation for her preaching. Parishioners and visitors alike noted the clarity, warmth, and accessibility of her sermons. She had a gift for connecting scripture to everyday life, for drawing out theological insights without losing touch with the lived experiences of her congregation. This ability to bridge the gap between ancient tradition and modern relevance would become one of her hallmarks as a leader in the Church of England.

4.2 Pastoral Work and Community Engagement

If parish ministry introduced Sarah Mullally to the rhythms of church life, pastoral work and community engagement deepened her vocation. Her years as a nurse had already given her a profound understanding of human vulnerability, suffering, and resilience. In parish settings, she translated those skills into pastoral care that was both deeply personal and broadly community-focused.

Pastoral ministry, at its core, is about presence. It is about showing up in the moments when people feel most alone — at hospital bedsides, in prison visiting rooms, in the aftermath of tragedy. Mullally approached this work not as a professional obligation but as a calling. She carried into these encounters the same gentleness and compassion that had made her an effective nurse, but now imbued with theological depth and sacramental presence. For her, pastoral care was not just about comfort, but about bearing witness to God's love in the midst of human struggle.

Her engagement extended beyond the walls of the parish church. Mullally understood that the Church of England, as the established church, had a unique responsibility to serve the whole community, not just regular worshippers. She became actively involved in local schools, forging partnerships with teachers, students, and families. She participated in community development projects, working alongside civic leaders to address issues such as poverty, homelessness, and social exclusion. In every setting, she embodied the principle that faith must be lived out in action, that the gospel must be proclaimed not only in words but in deeds.

One of the most distinctive features of her pastoral approach was her inclusivity. She welcomed those who felt marginalized or alienated by the Church, whether because of gender, sexuality, social status, or personal history. She did not water down her faith, but she sought to embody it in ways that were hospitable rather than judgmental. This balance of conviction and compassion earned her the trust of people across diverse backgrounds.

Her community engagement also revealed her capacity as a bridge-builder. She had the ability to bring together groups that might otherwise remain isolated — church members and secular organizations, young people and the elderly, newcomers and long-standing residents. Her leadership style was collaborative, rooted in the conviction that every person had gifts to offer and a role to play in the flourishing of the community.

Through these experiences, Mullally began to emerge as more than a local parish priest. She was becoming recognized as a leader who could engage with complex social realities while remaining grounded in pastoral care. Her capacity to integrate faith with action, spirituality with social responsibility, marked her out as someone with a distinctive and needed voice in the wider Church.

4.3 Growing Recognition and Responsibility

As Sarah Mullally's ministry matured, her gifts could not remain hidden. Both parishioners and church leaders began to recognize that she had a unique combination of skills, experiences, and spiritual depth that equipped her for wider responsibilities.

Her background in healthcare leadership gave her a credibility that extended beyond the church community. She was accustomed to navigating complex institutions, managing large teams, and making decisions under pressure. In an era when the Church of England was increasingly required to engage with political, social, and economic challenges, these skills were invaluable.

Her preaching and teaching also began to attract wider attention. Invitations to speak at conferences, diocesan gatherings, and public events multiplied. Audiences resonated with her ability to articulate faith in a way that was both intellectually rigorous and practically relevant. She did not shy away from difficult topics, but addressed them with honesty, humility, and hope.

This growing recognition inevitably led to greater responsibility. She was entrusted with diocesan roles that required oversight of clergy, development of pastoral strategies, and leadership in areas such as mission, training, and governance. She proved adept at balancing the demands of these roles with her ongoing commitments to parish and community life.

Her leadership style was consistently collaborative. Rather than imposing her own agenda, she sought to empower others, to draw out their gifts, and to foster shared ownership of ministry. This approach reflected her conviction that leadership in the Church is not about power but about service. It also reflected her theological understanding of the body of Christ, in which every member has a role to play.

During this period, she also became increasingly involved in national conversations about the future of the Church of England. She participated in debates about the role of women in ministry, the church's response to social issues, and the need for renewal in worship and mission. Her contributions were marked by a rare combination of courage and humility — courage to speak truthfully, and humility to listen carefully.

It was becoming clear that Sarah Mullally was not just a parish priest or diocesan leader, but a figure of national significance. Her journey of recognition was not driven by ambition but by faithfulness. She did not seek leadership for its own sake, but responded to the opportunities and responsibilities that came her way with integrity and trust in God's guidance.

4.4 The Call to Greater Leadership

The final stage of this chapter in Sarah Mullally's story is the call to greater leadership — a call that would eventually lead her to the episcopate. Yet even before her appointment as a bishop, there were signs that her ministry was moving in this direction.

The Church of England was entering a period of transition. Questions of inclusivity, authority, and mission were becoming more urgent. The role of women in leadership was a particularly contested issue, with strong voices on both sides. In this context, the presence of leaders who could embody both competence and compassion, conviction and bridge-building, was vital.

Mullally's ministry had already demonstrated these qualities. She had shown that she could lead with integrity, that she could engage constructively with controversy, and that she could inspire trust across diverse communities. She was also unafraid of challenge. Having navigated the complexities of the NHS, she was not daunted by the institutional challenges of the Church.

When the call to greater leadership came, it was both surprising and inevitable. Surprising because she had not pursued it as a personal ambition. Inevitable because her gifts, experiences, and character had prepared her for such a role. The Church recognized in her a leader who could carry its hopes and navigate its challenges.

Her response to this call was consistent with the rest of her journey: one of faithfulness, humility, and trust. She did not see leadership as an elevation but as a deepening of service. For her, to lead was to serve at a greater scale, to bear responsibility not only for a parish or a community but for the wider life of the Church.

This call to greater leadership would culminate in her consecration as Bishop of Crediton and, later, as Bishop of London. But even before those milestones, the foundations had been laid in her years of parish ministry, pastoral care, community engagement, and growing recognition. Those experiences shaped her into the kind of leader the Church of England needed — one who could embody tradition and innovation, authority and humility, faith and action.

Sarah Mullally's years of serving the Church of England before her episcopal appointments reveal a story of faith lived out in ordinary yet profound ways. From the intimacy of parish ministry to the complexity of diocesan leadership, from the quiet presence at a hospital bedside to the public voice in national debates, she consistently demonstrated what it means to lead as a servant.

Her journey reminds us that true leadership does not begin with titles or positions. It begins with faithfulness in small things, with attentiveness to the people and communities entrusted to one's care. It is forged in the crucible of pastoral encounters, community challenges, and personal sacrifice. For Sarah Mullally, it was precisely these experiences that prepared her for the extraordinary responsibilities that lay ahead.

The Church of England, in recognizing her gifts and calling her to greater leadership, affirmed not only her personal vocation but also the broader truth that leadership is about service, that authority is about responsibility, and that faith, when lived authentically, can transform both individuals and institutions.

Chapter 5

Bishop of Crediton

When Sarah Mullally was consecrated as the Bishop of Crediton in 2015, it was more than a personal milestone. It was a historic and symbolic moment for the Church of England, a clear signal of the institution's slow but steady evolution in embracing female leadership at the highest levels. The appointment placed her in a position of visibility, responsibility, and influence that went far beyond the quiet rural beauty of Devon, the diocese she was called to serve. For many, her installation represented not only the recognition of her abilities but also the validation of years of advocacy for equality within the Church. For Mullally herself, the step was both exhilarating and sobering—a new chapter in her journey of faith, marked by challenges that tested her resilience and opportunities that allowed her to redefine what episcopal leadership could look like in the modern age.

In this chapter, we will explore Sarah Mullally's first steps in episcopacy through four lenses: the reactions surrounding her appointment, the particular challenges and opportunities she encountered in Devon, the shaping of her leadership style as a bishop, and her commitment to strengthening local church communities.

5.1 Appointment and Reactions

When news broke in October 2015 that Sarah Mullally would be the next Bishop of Crediton, part of the Diocese of Exeter, reactions were swift and layered with meaning. The Church of England had only recently approved the ordination of women to the episcopate in 2014, and Mullally's appointment as a bishop represented one of the early fruits of that decision. While she was not the first woman to be appointed a bishop—Libby Lane had that distinction as the Bishop of Stockport—Mullally's background and reputation made her appointment particularly significant.

First, she was already a figure of national importance due to her earlier career as Chief Nursing Officer for England, the highest nursing position in the country. This made her the first person in centuries to bring to the episcopate such a distinguished background outside of traditional church ministry. Her public service credentials and her reputation as a compassionate, yet firm, leader in healthcare lent her appointment a unique weight. The Church was not only elevating a woman but also someone whose leadership had been proven in the demanding world of the National Health Service.

The media framed the appointment as both progressive and practical. Newspapers celebrated the "trailblazing nurse-turned-bishop" and highlighted her unusual path to the episcopate. For secular audiences often skeptical of church hierarchies, the story of a modern woman who had excelled in one of the most challenging public professions before entering the priesthood was compelling.

Within the Church, the reactions were more complex. Supporters of women's ministry hailed her appointment as another confirmation that the Church of England was at last catching up with contemporary society. The Diocese of Exeter, traditionally rural and with a mix of progressive and conservative parishes, found itself at the center of a historic moment. Many clergy and lay members expressed joy at the news, speaking of her reputation for listening deeply, leading humbly, and balancing compassion with decisiveness.

However, not all responses were celebratory. As with other female appointments, a minority of traditionalists and Anglo-Catholics within the Church voiced discomfort or outright opposition. Some parishioners in Devon were uncertain about what a woman bishop would mean for them, particularly in communities where theological conservatism held sway. Yet even many of these skeptics noted her pastoral warmth and her proven ability to engage respectfully across divides.

For Mullally, the appointment came with mixed emotions. On one hand, it was a profound honor and responsibility. On the other hand, she understood the symbolic expectations placed upon her—she would be scrutinized not simply as a bishop, but as a woman bishop, as a public figure from outside the usual clerical mold, and as a leader charged with navigating a diocese of both rural parishes and urban challenges.

Her consecration at Canterbury Cathedral was marked with dignity and gravity. As she processed into the ancient cathedral, she carried not just her own calling but also the weight of countless women whose ministry had paved the way for her. For those present, it was an unforgettable moment, emblematic of a Church inching toward greater inclusivity while remaining rooted in tradition.

5.2 Challenges and Opportunities in Devon

Stepping into her role, Sarah Mullally quickly discovered that serving as Bishop of Crediton was both a privilege and a testing ground. The Diocese of Exeter covers the entire county of Devon, a region known for its stunning coastlines, rolling countryside, and deep historical ties to Christianity. While picturesque, the diocese carried with it a set of challenges that were as complex as they were distinctive.

Rural Communities and Sparse Congregations

One of the central challenges was the rural nature of much of Devon. Many parishes were small, spread out, and often struggling with dwindling attendance. Rural ministry brought its own pressures: fewer clergy to cover larger geographic areas, financial difficulties in maintaining historic church buildings, and a pervasive sense of marginalization in a society increasingly centered on cities.

Mullally quickly recognized the need to affirm the value of rural churches while also exploring creative ways to sustain ministry in such areas. She became a vocal advocate for the idea that small congregations, though limited in numbers, were vital witnesses to the presence of God in their communities. Her healthcare background helped her appreciate the importance of small, local networks—just as every community needs a nurse or doctor, every village could benefit from a visible, living expression of faith.

Economic and Social Inequalities

Devon, for all its beauty, was a county marked by contrasts. Tourism brought wealth to certain areas, while others suffered from economic decline, poor infrastructure, and limited opportunities for young people. Rural poverty, often hidden behind idyllic landscapes, was a real and pressing issue. As bishop, Mullally had to engage not only with the spiritual needs of her communities but also with their social struggles.

Her experience in public health proved invaluable here. She understood how deprivation affected families, mental health, and community cohesion. She advocated for the Church to play a role in alleviating these pressures, from food banks to social outreach programs, positioning the diocese as a moral voice in addressing inequality.

Traditionalism and Theological Division

As one of the early female bishops, Mullally also encountered theological opposition. Some parishes within the Diocese of Exeter held firmly to traditionalist teachings that resisted women's ordination. For these communities, the presence of a woman bishop was deeply challenging.

Rather than confrontational rhetoric, Mullally chose a path of dialogue and patience. She prioritized listening, meeting clergy and laity where they were, and affirming their right to hold traditional beliefs even as she embodied change. This approach did not erase tensions, but it created a climate in which disagreement could coexist with mutual respect.

Opportunities for Innovation

Despite these challenges, her tenure also opened opportunities. Devon's vibrant diversity—tourism hubs, rural villages, coastal towns, and urban centers like Exeter and Plymouth—meant that the diocese was a microcosm of the wider Church's issues. If creative solutions could work here, they could serve as models for other dioceses.

She encouraged experimentation in worship, the development of lay leadership, and new forms of ministry. Her ability to draw upon her managerial skills from the NHS gave her confidence in organizing teams, delegating responsibilities, and encouraging collaboration between clergy and laypeople.

In Devon, Mullally found a proving ground. Every problem she faced forced her to refine her vision for what episcopal leadership should be: not a distant, authoritarian figure but a shepherd deeply present among the flock.

5.3 Shaping Leadership Style as a Bishop

Sarah Mullally's time as Bishop of Crediton was transformative not only for the communities she served but also for her own identity as a leader. Having led within the healthcare system and then served as a parish priest, she now found herself navigating the distinct demands of episcopal office. Through her actions and decisions, she gradually shaped a leadership style that would later define her tenure as Bishop of London.

Listening First, Leading Second

At the heart of Mullally's leadership was a commitment to listening. She often remarked that effective leadership required hearing the stories, concerns, and aspirations of those one was called to serve. She traveled extensively across Devon, visiting small parishes and rural congregations, meeting with clergy, and making herself visible in community settings.

This listening-first approach was more than symbolic. It allowed her to build trust with people who might otherwise have viewed her appointment with skepticism. In communities where tradition weighed heavily, her willingness to engage without judgment earned her respect. For clergy dealing with isolation or burnout, her attentive presence provided encouragement.

Collaboration and Team Building

Another hallmark of her leadership style was collaboration. Drawing upon her NHS experience— where multidisciplinary teams were crucial—Mullally valued the diverse gifts of clergy and laity. She resisted hierarchical models that placed all responsibility on the bishop and instead sought to empower others to take ownership of their ministries.

She encouraged lay leadership, particularly in rural parishes where full-time clergy were scarce. She also worked to strengthen diocesan teams, recognizing that complex challenges required collective wisdom. This collaborative model reflected her belief that the Church, like the body of Christ, flourishes when every part contributes.

Balancing Tradition and Innovation

Mullally also learned to navigate the delicate balance between tradition and innovation. She respected the liturgical richness and historical continuity of the Church of England, while also recognizing the need for fresh approaches that could speak to contemporary society.

For example, she supported creative worship initiatives that incorporated local culture or modern technology. At the same time, she defended the importance of maintaining sacred rhythms of prayer, scripture, and sacrament. This dual approach allowed her to bridge generational divides within the Church, engaging both younger audiences seeking relevance and older members valuing continuity.

Pastoral Care as a Core of Leadership

Perhaps most distinctive was her emphasis on pastoral care. For Mullally, leadership was not primarily about wielding authority but about tending to people's spiritual and emotional well-being. Her nursing background sharpened this perspective—just as a nurse tends to the whole person, so too a bishop must care for the whole community.

Stories abound of her visiting parishes where attendance was dwindling and morale was low, offering encouragement and practical support. She was known to write personal letters, pray with parishioners, and lend her presence to those struggling with illness or grief. This pastoral orientation grounded her leadership in compassion and authenticity.

Courage in the Face of Scrutiny

As one of the early female bishops, Mullally also had to cultivate courage. Every decision she made, every sermon she preached, and every public statement she gave was weighed not just on its own merits but as a reflection of women's capacity for episcopal leadership. The burden of representation was immense.

She approached this challenge with quiet determination. Rather than allowing herself to be defined by gender debates, she focused on her calling and responsibilities. By embodying steady, competent leadership, she gradually shifted perceptions. Her style was not confrontational but transformative in its consistency: she showed, by example, that a woman could lead with grace, authority, and effectiveness.

5.4 Strengthening Local Church Communities

Ultimately, Sarah Mullally's ministry in Devon was rooted in her commitment to strengthening local church communities. She believed that the vitality of the Church depended not only on diocesan strategies or episcopal leadership but on the flourishing of each parish, no matter how small or remote.

Reinvigorating Rural Parishes

She invested time and energy into rural parishes, encouraging them to see their size not as a weakness but as an opportunity for intimate, resilient community life. She reminded congregations that even a handful of faithful worshippers could be a powerful witness. In doing so, she pushed against a culture that equated success only with large numbers.

She supported the development of shared ministry models, where several parishes worked together under the leadership of one or two clergy, supplemented by lay ministers. This approach helped ensure sustainability while fostering cooperation among communities that might otherwise feel isolated.

Encouraging Lay Ministry

Mullally consistently emphasized that ministry was not the sole responsibility of ordained clergy. She championed lay ministry as a vital part of the Church's mission. Through training programs and support structures, she encouraged ordinary Christians to step into roles of leadership, whether in worship, pastoral care, or community outreach.

This emphasis democratized the Church's mission. It affirmed that every member had a part to play in building

God's kingdom and helped parishes to grow less dependent on overstretched clergy.

Social Outreach and Witness

She also worked to strengthen the Church's witness in addressing social issues. Food poverty, loneliness, and mental health were particular concerns in Devon, and Mullally encouraged parishes to respond with compassion and practical action. Under her guidance, many churches expanded food banks, developed programs for the elderly, and created safe spaces for those struggling with isolation.

In this way, she positioned the Church not just as a spiritual haven but as a vital part of the social fabric. By meeting people's tangible needs, parishes demonstrated the relevance of faith in everyday life.

Fostering Unity Amid Diversity

Another part of strengthening local communities was her commitment to unity amid theological diversity. She recognized that disagreements over issues such as women's ordination or sexuality could fracture parishes. Rather than imposing uniformity, she sought to create spaces where people could disagree without division.

Her ability to listen deeply, respect differing convictions, and model humility helped many communities navigate these tensions. She encouraged clergy and laity alike to focus on what united them—their shared faith in Christ—rather than what divided them.

Sarah Mullally's time as Bishop of Crediton was brief in years but rich in impact. It was a period in which she took her first steps as a bishop, confronted challenges unique to Devon, refined a distinctive style of leadership, and strengthened local church communities in ways that would ripple outward long after her departure.

For Mullally, the role was both preparation and proving ground. It tested her ability to translate her gifts from healthcare and parish ministry into episcopal leadership. It taught her how to listen across divides, balance tradition with innovation, and care for communities both fragile and strong.

Most importantly, it demonstrated that episcopacy in the twenty-first century could be both rooted in ancient faith and responsive to modern realities. Her work in Devon was not just about sustaining churches; it was about breathing new life into them, showing that leadership grounded in compassion, humility, and courage could transform even the most challenging contexts.

By the time she was later called to serve as Bishop of London, Sarah Mullally had already shown in Crediton what kind of leader she was: a listener, a collaborator, a pastor, and a visionary. Devon had been her first steps in episcopacy—but for the Church of England, those steps marked the beginning of a larger journey toward renewal and inclusion.

Chapter 6

The Historic Appointment as Bishop of London

When history shifts, it does not always announce itself with fanfare. Sometimes, it moves quietly, almost imperceptibly, until a single appointment, decision, or act reveals the enormity of what has changed. Sarah Mullally's appointment as the Bishop of London in 2017 was one of those moments—a turning point in the story of the Church of England, in the story of women in leadership, and in the personal journey of a woman who had already lived two extraordinary lives: first as a nurse and then as a priest.

The Bishop of London is no ordinary office. It is the third most senior position in the Church of England, behind only the Archbishops of Canterbury and York. It is a seat that carries with it centuries of tradition, a staggering weight of responsibility, and a visibility that stretches far beyond the confines of ecclesiastical life. For centuries, it had been occupied exclusively by men. With Sarah Mullally's appointment, that narrative changed.

Her rise was not only a personal milestone but a cultural, religious, and symbolic moment that reverberated across Britain and beyond. This chapter explores in detail how she broke centuries of tradition, how the public and the media responded, what it means to lead a diocese as globally significant as London, and what her appointment has meant—both in practice and in symbolism—for women in the Church.

6.1 Breaking Centuries of Tradition

For nearly 1,500 years, the Diocese of London had been governed by men. From its earliest medieval bishops, through the turbulence of the English Reformation, and into the modern age, the role had been a symbol of continuity in an ever-changing world. The idea of a woman sitting on the episcopal throne of St. Paul's Cathedral was, until very recently, unthinkable.

The Church of England had only approved the ordination of women to the priesthood in 1992, and it took until 1994 for the first women to be ordained. Even then, the road to women's full participation in leadership was long and contested. The debate over women bishops dragged on for decades, marked by theological disputes, synod votes, and passionate advocacy both for and against. When, in 2014, the Church of England finally approved the consecration of women bishops, it marked a watershed moment.

The appointment of Sarah Mullally as Bishop of London just three years later was not simply the application of that decision; it was its most powerful realization yet. London was not just another diocese. It was the heart of the nation's capital, a global crossroads, and the spiritual seat of one of the most iconic cathedrals in the world: St. Paul's. The symbolic power of this diocese was immense, and to place a woman at its helm was to declare, in the most visible way possible, that the Church of England was changing.

Sarah's appointment was historic not only because of her gender but also because of her background. Unlike many of her predecessors, she had not risen through the traditional ranks of academia or ecclesiastical hierarchy. Her formative career was in healthcare, where she had risen to the highest levels of leadership as Chief Nursing Officer for England. She brought with her a wealth of experience in management, policy, and frontline care—skills that set her apart from her peers and made her uniquely suited for the challenges of modern episcopacy.

When her appointment was formally announced in December 2017, the news carried with it both astonishment and admiration. Many could hardly believe that, so soon after the ordination of women bishops had been approved, one of the most senior and visible posts in the Church had gone to a woman.

But there was also a deeper symbolism at play. By appointing Sarah Mullally, the Church was not simply following its own internal reforms. It was sending a signal to society at large. The Church of England—an institution often accused of being slow, traditionalist, and resistant to change—was capable of bold, progressive action. It was capable of breaking its own centuries-old patterns and opening its most senior leadership roles to women.

Her installation was a moment of profound symbolism. The image of Sarah Mullally walking into St. Paul's Cathedral, vested as bishop and ready to take up her role, stood as a visual marker of the end of one era and the beginning of another. The stained-glass ceilings of the Church of England, cracked open in 2014, were now being shattered in its very heart.

6.2 Public Response and Media Attention

The public and media response to Sarah Mullally's appointment was immediate and intense. Newspapers across the United Kingdom and beyond carried headlines announcing the historic decision. The BBC, The Guardian, The Times, and countless other outlets published stories highlighting the breakthrough moment.

For many, it was a cause for celebration. Advocates of gender equality in the Church hailed the appointment as a long-overdue recognition of women's gifts and leadership. Congregations across the country, particularly those with female clergy, saw it as a source of encouragement and inspiration. Here, at last, was visible proof that the Church of England was beginning to reflect the diversity of its people.

Yet the response was not uniformly positive. Within the Church, there remained groups and individuals who opposed the ordination of women, particularly in leadership roles. For them, the appointment of a female Bishop of London was troubling. Some traditionalists expressed dismay, citing theological reasons for their opposition. They argued that the Church was straying from scripture and tradition, and they questioned whether this appointment could deepen existing divisions within the Anglican Communion.

The media coverage captured both sides of the debate. Headlines often emphasized the historic nature of the appointment, but they also noted the challenges Sarah would face in uniting a diocese as diverse and sometimes divided as London. The Church of England was, at the time, navigating ongoing debates around gender, sexuality, and doctrine. Sarah's appointment, though groundbreaking, placed her at the center of these conversations.

Public curiosity also turned toward her personal story. Journalists revisited her career as a nurse and as England's Chief Nursing Officer, marveling at her transition into church leadership. Interviews highlighted her compassion, her managerial skill, and her unflappable calm. She was portrayed as someone who could navigate complexity with grace—an image that contrasted sharply with some of the more combative personalities often seen in ecclesiastical debates.

What made Sarah particularly compelling to the public was her ability to connect the spiritual with the practical. She spoke often about care, compassion, and service—values that resonated far beyond the Church. In a Britain where religious affiliation was declining, she embodied a form of leadership that was accessible and grounded. She was not merely a theologian speaking in abstract terms; she was a former nurse who had spent nights on hospital wards, who had comforted patients in pain, and who had led in crises.

Her appointment also attracted international attention. The global Anglican Communion watched closely, as did churches in other denominations. For many women in the wider Christian world, Sarah's appointment served as a beacon of possibility. If the Bishop of London could be a woman, then perhaps their own churches could imagine similar breakthroughs.

The mixed reactions reflected the broader tensions within the Church and society. Yet the very intensity of the response underscored just how significant her appointment was. It was not a marginal change. It was a headline-grabbing, paradigm-shifting moment that placed the Church of England in the center of public debate and imagination.

6.3 The Weight of Leadership in a Global City

To understand the enormity of Sarah Mullally's appointment, one must appreciate the role of the Bishop of London. The Diocese of London is one of the largest and most complex in the Church of England. It encompasses not only the historic and financial heart of the nation but also some of its most diverse and rapidly changing communities.

Leading the Diocese of London means presiding over an extraordinary spectrum of parishes. At one end are historic churches like St. Paul's Cathedral, whose influence and symbolism extend worldwide. At the other are small, local parishes embedded in multicultural neighborhoods, each with its own challenges and opportunities. The bishop must be equally comfortable delivering state sermons at grand occasions and sitting in a modest parish hall listening to the concerns of immigrant families or struggling communities.

The role also carries a unique national and international profile. The Bishop of London is often called upon to speak on issues of public importance, from social justice and healthcare to immigration and education. In times of national crisis, such as terrorist attacks or natural disasters, the Bishop of London is expected to be a pastoral presence and a voice of reassurance.

For Sarah Mullally, this meant carrying a dual weight: the ordinary challenges of leadership in a vast and diverse diocese, and the extraordinary scrutiny of being the first woman ever to occupy the role. Every decision she made, every sermon she preached, and every appearance she gave was subject to heightened attention. Supporters and critics alike watched closely, interpreting her actions not only as her own but as a reflection of what it meant to have a woman in this position.

She approached the role with a balance of humility and resolve. Drawing on her background in nursing, she spoke often about listening—listening to parishes, to communities, and to those who felt unheard. She emphasized collaboration and dialogue, aware that the diocese's strength lay in its diversity. She also framed her leadership in terms of service, echoing both her healthcare career and her theological conviction that leadership in the Church is fundamentally about serving others.

But the challenges were real. London is a city marked by extremes—wealth and poverty, tradition and modernity, faith and secularism. The Church of England in London faces declining attendance in some areas while experiencing growth in others, particularly among immigrant congregations. It wrestles with theological divisions over gender and sexuality, as well as with the broader question of how to remain relevant in an increasingly secular society.

To carry the weight of leadership in such a context requires not only administrative skill but also moral and spiritual depth. Sarah Mullally's task was to embody the Church's presence in the capital in a way that spoke to both believers and skeptics, to both traditionalists and progressives. She had to hold together a diocese that mirrored the complexities of the city itself.

Her leadership style, characterized by compassion, inclusivity, and steadiness, became her greatest asset. She did not try to impose uniformity on the diocese; instead, she sought to nurture dialogue, foster respect, and model what it meant to live faithfully amid difference. In doing so, she demonstrated that the weight of leadership, though immense, could be carried with grace.

6.4 What This Appointment Meant for Women in the Church

Perhaps the most profound significance of Sarah Mullally's appointment lay in what it represented for women in the Church of England. For centuries, women had been excluded from leadership, their gifts often unrecognized or underutilized. The ordination of women as priests in the 1990s had been a major breakthrough, but many argued that true equality could not be realized until women could occupy the highest offices of the Church.

By becoming Bishop of London, Sarah Mullally became not only a leader but also a symbol. She embodied the possibility of women exercising authority at the very highest levels of the Church. Her presence in St. Paul's

Cathedral was a visible, undeniable reminder that women could lead, could teach, could govern, and could inspire.

For female clergy, her appointment was a source of deep encouragement. Many spoke of the sense of validation and empowerment they felt. No longer were they simply tolerated in leadership roles; they now had a visible role model at the pinnacle of ecclesiastical power. For young women discerning a call to ministry, Sarah's example opened doors of imagination. They could now aspire to roles that, only a few years earlier, had been closed to them.

But the significance went beyond the Church. In a society still grappling with issues of gender equality, her appointment sent a message about the kind of leadership women could provide. She demonstrated that leadership is not defined by gender but by character, skill, and vision. Her calm authority, her experience in both healthcare and ministry, and her commitment to service challenged stereotypes about what women leaders could be.

At the same time, her appointment did not erase the challenges that women continued to face. There were still opponents within the Church who resisted female leadership. There were still glass ceilings, both visible and invisible, in many institutions. But Sarah's appointment marked a decisive step forward. It showed that change was not only possible but already underway.

Her appointment also had ecumenical and international implications. In the wider Anglican Communion, the ordination of women remained a contentious issue, with some provinces embracing it and others rejecting it. Sarah's role as Bishop of London, one of the most visible dioceses in the global Anglican family, placed the question of women's leadership firmly in the spotlight. Her effectiveness in the role became a living argument for the value of women in episcopal ministry.

Ultimately, what her appointment meant for women in the Church can be summed up in one word: possibility. It expanded the horizon of what could be imagined and achieved. It stood as a living example that centuries of exclusion could be overcome, that tradition could evolve, and that leadership could be redefined in ways that included rather than excluded.

The appointment of Sarah Mullally as Bishop of London was more than a personal milestone. It was a turning point in the life of the Church of England and a moment of profound cultural significance. It broke centuries of tradition, sparked public debate, placed her at the center of national and international attention, and redefined what leadership could look like in the Church.

For the Church, it was a statement of change. For society, it was a sign of progress. For women, it was a moment of inspiration and empowerment. And for Sarah herself, it was the continuation of a journey marked by service, compassion, and courage.

In her appointment, history shifted. The Church of England stepped into a new era, carrying with it both the challenges of the present and the hopes of the future. And at the heart of that shift stood Sarah Mullally, a woman who had already given her life to service and who now bore the responsibility of leading one of the most significant dioceses in the Christian world.

Chapter 7

Leading in the 21st Century

The 21st century is an age of paradox. It is at once an era of rapid technological advancement, unparalleled connectivity, and cultural pluralism, while also being a time of deep social fragmentation, political polarization, and spiritual uncertainty. For the Church of England, and particularly for its senior leaders, these tensions manifest daily. At the heart of this dynamic stands the Bishop of London, an office second only to the Archbishop of Canterbury in influence and responsibility. Sarah Mullally's appointment to this role in 2018 placed her in a position where her faith, experience, and character would be tested not only by tradition but by the evolving demands of modern Britain.

To lead in the 21st century is to balance continuity with change, sacred tradition with contemporary relevance, and pastoral care with prophetic challenge. In this chapter, we will explore how Sarah Mullally has inhabited this role: what it means to serve as Bishop of London, the challenges facing the Church of England in our time, the advocacy she has brought for diversity and inclusion, and the way she has positioned faith in dialogue with wider society and politics.

7.1 The Role of the Bishop of London

The Bishop of London occupies a unique place within both the Church of England and British society. Unlike other episcopal roles, this office comes with not only spiritual responsibilities but also civic, political, and cultural dimensions. The Diocese of London is vast, diverse, and highly visible; it includes some of the most historic cathedrals, parishes, and religious institutions in the country, as well as the bustling cosmopolitan communities that make up the capital.

Traditionally, the Bishop of London has acted as a bridge between the church and the state. London's historical role as the seat of government and commerce means that the bishop often stands at the crossroads of religious influence and civic responsibility. From officiating at state occasions to participating in national debates, the bishop's voice carries weight well beyond church walls.

For Sarah Mullally, the role has carried both symbolic and practical significance. Symbolically, her appointment as the first woman to hold the office represented a seismic moment in Anglican history, signaling a shift towards greater gender equality in leadership. Practically, her duties range from overseeing hundreds of clergy and parishes across the diocese to representing the Church of England in matters of national importance.

Her nursing background adds an unusual but invaluable dimension to this office. Unlike predecessors who came through more traditional clerical paths, Mullally approaches leadership with the mindset of a practitioner accustomed to managing complex systems, responding to crises, and placing human dignity at the center of her decisions. The Bishop of London is expected to be pastor, administrator, diplomat, and theologian in equal measure. Mullally's life experience has allowed her to navigate these overlapping responsibilities with a rare blend of empathy and pragmatism.

The role also carries ceremonial and liturgical duties. The Bishop of London presides over St Paul's Cathedral, a national symbol where royal services, commemorations, and civic gatherings are held. From leading services for state funerals to offering prayers during national emergencies, the bishop's voice often echoes at moments when the nation looks for reassurance and meaning. Mullally has embraced this aspect with characteristic humility, understanding that such occasions are opportunities to bring faith into the heart of public life.

Yet the role is not confined to grandeur. At its core, it is deeply pastoral. The Bishop of London is responsible for the wellbeing of clergy, the growth of parishes, and the spiritual flourishing of diverse communities. In a diocese where some congregations thrive with thousands of worshippers while others struggle for survival, Mullally's leadership requires a balance of vision, strategic planning, and genuine pastoral care.

7.2 Modern Challenges Facing the Church of England

To understand Sarah Mullally's leadership, one must also confront the reality of the challenges she faces. The Church of England, as the established church, carries both privilege and burden. Its history is deeply interwoven with the life of the nation, but its relevance in the modern age is often questioned.

One of the most pressing challenges is declining attendance. Across much of the United Kingdom, regular churchgoing has diminished, particularly among younger generations. While London shows pockets of growth due to its international diversity, overall numbers reflect a broader trend of secularization. For Mullally, this reality demands not despair but creative engagement. She has often spoken of the need for the church to reimagine itself, to be present in communities where traditional parish models no longer suffice, and to make faith accessible without diluting its depth.

Another challenge lies in cultural diversity. London is one of the most multicultural cities in the world. The diocese includes communities from every corner of the globe, bringing with them different Christian traditions, expressions of faith, and cultural expectations. This diversity is both a gift and a challenge. It enriches worship and community life but also requires sensitive leadership to ensure unity without erasing difference. Mullally's style has been to listen, learn, and encourage dialogue, creating space for communities to flourish while remaining connected to the broader identity of the Church of England.

The church also grapples with issues of credibility and trust. Past failures, particularly in safeguarding and responses to abuse, have left deep wounds. For leaders like Mullally, addressing these failures with transparency, humility, and firm action is paramount. Her background in healthcare, where accountability and safeguarding are non-negotiable, has equipped her to approach this area with seriousness and resolve.

A further challenge is the rapid pace of societal change. Questions around gender identity, sexuality, climate justice, and economic inequality dominate public discourse, and the church cannot ignore them. While some within the church resist engaging with these issues, Mullally has emphasized the need for the church to be present in the conversations that shape society. To her, the gospel demands engagement, not withdrawal.

Finally, the Church of England must navigate the tension between tradition and modernity. Its liturgy, sacraments, and structures carry centuries of continuity, yet it must also adapt to the needs of people who communicate through digital platforms, live in multicultural neighborhoods, and often approach spirituality outside institutional frameworks. Leading in such a landscape requires both fidelity to the faith's core and courage to innovate—a balance Mullally constantly seeks.

7.3 Advocacy for Diversity, Inclusion, and Renewal

Perhaps one of Sarah Mullally's most significant contributions as Bishop of London has been her advocacy for diversity and inclusion. Her own appointment was itself a landmark for gender equality in the Church of England. But Mullally has not stopped at being a symbol; she has actively worked to open doors for others and to ensure that the church reflects the full breadth of its people.

On gender equality, she has been a tireless advocate for women in leadership. While women now serve as priests and bishops, their full acceptance in some areas of the church remains contested. Mullally has approached these tensions not with confrontation but with a steady insistence on equality, rooted in both theology and practice. She embodies the conviction that the gifts of women are not optional but essential to the life of the church.

Her advocacy also extends to racial and cultural diversity. London's congregations include significant numbers of Christians from African, Caribbean, Asian, and Latin

American backgrounds. These communities often bring vitality, growth, and deep faith traditions. Mullally has worked to ensure that leadership structures within the diocese reflect this reality, resisting the temptation to maintain a monocultural identity in a multicultural city. She has encouraged recruitment, mentorship, and representation at every level, knowing that symbolic gestures are not enough—systemic change is required.

In matters of sexuality and inclusion, Mullally has had to navigate one of the most divisive debates within the Anglican Communion. While the church as a whole remains divided on issues such as same-sex marriage, she has consistently emphasized the importance of listening, respect, and pastoral care. Her approach is marked by compassion: even when official policies remain contested, she insists that all people are welcomed and valued in the church. For Mullally, inclusion is not merely about policy but about lived experience—the assurance that no one is outside the reach of God's love.

Beyond issues of identity, Mullally has been an advocate for renewal in how the church engages with society. She has called for imaginative approaches to evangelism, greater use of digital media, and fresh expressions of church that meet people where they are. For her, inclusion means more than who is allowed at the altar; it also means creating spaces where people unfamiliar with church culture can encounter faith in ways that are authentic and relevant.

This advocacy is not without resistance. Critics sometimes accuse her of being too progressive or too cautious, depending on their perspective. Yet her leadership is rooted in a conviction that diversity and inclusion are not political trends but gospel imperatives. She consistently frames her advocacy not in secular terms but in the language of Christian discipleship: to follow Christ is to break down barriers, to welcome the stranger, and to seek justice for the marginalized.

7.4 Faith in Dialogue with Society and Politics

The role of the Bishop of London is not confined to the internal life of the church. It necessarily involves dialogue with society and politics, especially in a capital city where every major issue of national importance converges. Mullally has embraced this responsibility with careful balance, recognizing both the opportunities and the sensitivities involved.

On political issues, she has avoided partisanship, understanding that the church must speak to all people, not align with particular parties. Yet she has not shied away from moral leadership. On matters such as poverty, healthcare, housing, and climate change, she has spoken with clarity, drawing from her background in nursing and her theological convictions. Her interventions often highlight the human cost of political decisions, grounding debate not in ideology but in compassion.

During moments of national crisis, such as the COVID-19 pandemic, Mullally's dual identity as nurse and bishop gave her a distinctive voice. She was able to articulate the anxieties of frontline workers while also offering spiritual support to a nation in distress. At St Paul's Cathedral and beyond, she led prayers, addressed grief, and reminded the public of hope in the midst of uncertainty. In doing so, she demonstrated how faith can provide not only private comfort but also public meaning.

Her dialogue with society also extends to interfaith engagement. London is home to vast Muslim, Jewish, Hindu, Sikh, Buddhist, and other communities. For the Bishop of London, interfaith relationships are not optional but essential to the city's wellbeing. Mullally has participated in joint initiatives, built relationships with other faith leaders, and consistently emphasized that peace and justice require collaboration across religious boundaries.

At the same time, she has engaged with cultural institutions—from the arts to academia—recognizing that the gospel must be heard in the language of contemporary culture. She has encouraged the church to participate in debates about ethics in technology, artificial intelligence, and bioethics, areas where her medical background lends her both authority and curiosity.

What marks her approach is a refusal to accept the false choice between faith and modernity. She does not see Christianity as an outdated tradition but as a living voice that can enrich the present. Her dialogue with society and politics is not defensive but invitational: she seeks to show that the wisdom of faith, when articulated humbly and authentically, has something vital to contribute to the common good.

To lead in the 21st century is to stand at a crossroads of history, faith, and society. For Sarah Mullally, the role of Bishop of London is not merely about maintaining an institution but about reimagining its place in a rapidly changing world. She carries the weight of tradition while also opening doors for renewal. She faces challenges of secularization, diversity, and division, yet she approaches them not with fear but with hope and determination.

Her leadership embodies the conviction that the church's relevance depends not on retreating from modernity but on engaging it with courage and compassion. By advocating for diversity, inclusion, and renewal, and by entering dialogue with society and politics, she has sought to model what it means for faith to be both timeless and timely.

In Sarah Mullally's story, we see not only the journey of one woman but the unfolding narrative of a church striving to find its voice in the 21st century. Her leadership is a reminder that even in times of uncertainty, faith can inspire, challenge, and transform both individuals and societies.

Chapter 8

Faith, Theology, and Vision

Sarah Mullally's story is not simply one of personal achievement or a career that spanned healthcare and the Church of England; it is, at its deepest level, the unfolding of a theological journey. Her faith, her understanding of scripture, and her vision for the Church of tomorrow are the pillars that have shaped her leadership and continue to define her legacy.

While many leaders within the Church of England have risen to prominence through years of ecclesiastical service, Mullally's route was unique. Having already stood at the pinnacle of the nursing profession as England's Chief Nursing Officer, she carried with her a lived experience of care, compassion, and resilience. That grounding was not abandoned when she entered ordained ministry—it became the foundation of her theology. Her vision of faith was never abstract, never detached from human suffering and healing. It was forged in the wards of hospitals, in the quiet moments of pastoral care, and in the conviction that the Church must embody Christ's love for the marginalized, the voiceless, and the brokenhearted.

This chapter explores the depth of her theological commitments, her interpretation of scripture and tradition, her careful but courageous voice as both pastor and prophet, and the wider vision she holds for Christianity in twenty-first century Britain.

8.1 Sarah Mullally's Theological Foundations

At the heart of Sarah Mullally's theology is a conviction that faith is not a separate sphere of life but the lifeblood that courses through every human endeavor. Her professional career in nursing was not a prelude to her vocation but an expression of it. When she speaks of caring for patients, she often frames it as a calling, a vocation in which God's love was mediated through compassion and healing.

Her theological foundation is therefore incarnational. She emphasizes that the God who became flesh in Jesus Christ is a God who steps into the reality of human suffering, not one who stands aloof from it. This incarnational theology runs like a thread through her ministry. To Mullally, the Church cannot be confined to liturgy or hierarchy; it must enter into the messiness of the world, bearing witness to Christ through action as much as through words.

A second key aspect of her foundation is service. Influenced by her Anglican heritage, she has often highlighted Christ's model of servant leadership— washing the feet of his disciples, identifying with the lowly, and giving his life for the world. For Mullally, leadership is not about power or prestige but about humility and service. This ethic of service was not only drawn from her Christian faith but also reinforced by her nursing background, where leadership often meant advocating for patients, guiding teams, and ensuring care for the vulnerable.

Her theological training, which followed her nursing career, deepened these convictions. She immersed herself in Anglican tradition, appreciating its breadth and capacity to hold together diverse theological perspectives. Unlike leaders who align rigidly with one camp, Mullally embodies the Anglican via media—the "middle way" that seeks balance between Protestant and Catholic elements, between scripture, tradition, and reason.

She has often emphasized the importance of contextual theology, recognizing that theology is not static but must be lived out in the shifting contexts of each generation. Yet she is also cautious, anchoring change in prayer, scripture, and discernment rather than in cultural trends alone. This makes her both deeply rooted and pastorally adaptable—a rare combination that underpins her approach to leadership.

Her foundations, then, are both deeply personal and firmly ecclesial. They are personal in that they flow from her lived experiences—her encounters with patients, families, and parishioners. They are ecclesial in that they are shaped by her deep respect for the Anglican tradition and its theological richness. Taken together, these elements define a theology that is both practical and profound: a theology of incarnation, service, and contextual faithfulness.

8.2 Her Understanding of Scripture and Tradition

For Sarah Mullally, scripture is not merely a text to be studied but a living word through which God continues to speak. Her approach to the Bible reflects both reverence and critical engagement. She affirms its authority as central to Christian life, but she also emphasizes the need for interpretation within the community, guided by tradition, reason, and the lived realities of faith.

She often points to the Gospels as her starting point. The stories of Jesus' healing, compassion, and challenge to societal norms are central to her ministry. The Gospel accounts of Jesus dining with tax collectors, touching lepers, and welcoming children are not simply stories of the past but mandates for the present. They compel the Church to prioritize inclusion, healing, and justice.

At the same time, she recognizes the complexity of scripture. She does not shy away from passages that challenge modern sensibilities. Instead, she approaches them with a hermeneutic of love, asking how these texts, when read in the light of Christ, can guide the Church toward faithfulness today. This approach reflects a hallmark of Anglican theology: scripture is interpreted within the wider framework of tradition and reason, ensuring that it remains both authoritative and relevant.

Tradition, for Mullally, is not a dead weight but a living inheritance. She values the richness of Anglican liturgy, the beauty of historic prayers, and the continuity of the Church across centuries. Yet she resists the temptation to idolize tradition, reminding others that tradition must serve the gospel rather than become an end in itself.

She embodies the Anglican principle of continuity-in-renewal. The Church must remain faithful to its creeds and core doctrines, yet it must also be willing to adapt its practices and structures to serve God's mission in each generation. This is particularly evident in her support for the ordination of women and her willingness to engage in complex discussions around sexuality, inclusion, and justice.

In her preaching, Mullally often weaves together scripture, tradition, and contemporary life. She does not present the Bible as a set of abstract principles but as a narrative that intersects with the stories of individuals and communities today. She draws on traditional Anglican rhythms of prayer and worship while also affirming the need for creative expressions that connect with younger generations and those on the margins of the Church.

Ultimately, her approach to scripture and tradition is both faithful and dynamic: faithful to the authority of God's word and the richness of the Church's heritage, yet dynamic in its openness to new insights, contexts, and voices.

8.3 The Balance of Pastoral Care and Prophetic Voice

One of Sarah Mullally's defining characteristics as a leader is her ability to hold together two roles that are often in tension: the pastor and the prophet. The pastoral role emphasizes compassion, listening, and support. The prophetic role demands courage, confrontation, and speaking uncomfortable truths.

Her nursing background trained her in pastoral sensitivity. She knows what it means to sit with someone in pain, to listen to stories of loss, and to accompany individuals through times of crisis. This capacity for empathy carries into her ministry, where she is known for her gentleness, approachability, and attentiveness. Parishioners, clergy, and colleagues often describe her as someone who makes space for people to be heard and valued.

Yet she does not allow pastoral sensitivity to become avoidance of difficult issues. She also carries a prophetic edge, willing to challenge the Church and society when necessary. She has spoken boldly about gender equality, the need for inclusion, and the dangers of clinging to outdated structures. Her prophetic voice is not strident but firm; it arises from her conviction that the Church must reflect the justice and love of Christ.

The balance of pastoral and prophetic is evident in how she engages with controversial topics. On questions of sexuality, for example, she has sought to listen carefully to all sides, acknowledging the pain and convictions of those involved. At the same time, she calls the Church to deeper reflection on how it embodies God's inclusive love. She avoids simplistic answers, choosing instead to hold space for dialogue, prayer, and discernment.

This balance is also reflected in her leadership style. As Bishop of London, she faces the challenge of leading one of the most diverse dioceses in the Church of England. Her approach has been to prioritize listening, consultation, and collaboration, ensuring that all voices are heard. Yet when decisions must be made, she is willing to act with clarity and conviction, even if not everyone agrees.

This ability to be both pastor and prophet makes her leadership distinctive. Many leaders lean heavily toward one side—either comforting without challenging, or challenging without comforting. Mullally embodies both, showing that true leadership in the Church requires the gentleness of a shepherd and the courage of a prophet.

8.4 A Vision for the Future of Christianity in Britain

Perhaps the most compelling aspect of Sarah Mullally's theology is her vision for the Church's future. She does not view Christianity in Britain as a relic of the past, nor as a fortress to be defended against modernity. Instead, she envisions a Church that is outward-facing, engaged, and hopeful.

At the core of her vision is inclusion. She believes the Church must be a place where all are welcome, regardless of background, gender, or social status. This does not mean abandoning doctrine but embodying the radical hospitality of Jesus. She often highlights the image of the banquet table, where the marginalized and overlooked are given places of honor.

She also envisions a Church that is engaged with society's challenges. Whether addressing issues of poverty, inequality, mental health, or climate change, she insists that the Church must be present in the public square, offering both practical support and moral guidance. Her own background in healthcare has given her a particular sensitivity to issues of health and well-being, and she continues to advocate for the Church's role in promoting holistic human flourishing.

Another key element of her vision is adaptability. She recognizes that traditional forms of church are struggling to connect with new generations. While she values historic liturgy, she also champions creative expressions of worship and community life that can reach those unfamiliar with church culture. She supports fresh expressions of church, digital engagement, and new forms of discipleship that meet people where they are.

For Mullally, the future of Christianity in Britain also depends on leadership that reflects the diversity of the nation. She has been a trailblazer as the first female Bishop of London, and she continues to encourage the development of women and minority leaders in the Church. Her vision is not only of a more inclusive Church but also of a more representative one, where leadership mirrors the diversity of God's people.

Underlying all these elements is her conviction that the Church's mission is to bear witness to Christ in word and deed. She envisions a Church that is not obsessed with institutional survival but committed to faithful discipleship. In her view, the measure of the Church's success is not the size of its congregations but the depth of its love, the authenticity of its witness, and its impact on the lives of those around it.

Her vision is neither naive nor pessimistic. She acknowledges the challenges the Church faces— declining attendance, cultural marginalization, and internal divisions. Yet she approaches these challenges with hope, grounded in her belief that God is still at work in Britain. She often reminds others that resurrection is at the heart of the Christian story: even when things seem bleak, God brings new life.

Sarah Mullally's faith, theology, and vision reflect a leader deeply grounded in tradition yet courageously open to the future. Her foundations are incarnational and servant-hearted, rooted in both her healthcare background and her theological training. Her understanding of scripture and tradition combines reverence with adaptability, ensuring faithfulness without rigidity. Her balance of pastoral care and prophetic voice makes her a compassionate yet courageous leader. And her vision for the future of Christianity in Britain is inclusive, engaged, and hopeful.

In an era when many question the relevance of the Church, Mullally offers a vision of faith that is deeply human and deeply divine: a faith that touches the suffering, challenges injustice, and dares to hope for resurrection. She reminds the Church that its calling is not to retreat from the world but to enter into it with the love of Christ—healing, serving, and bearing witness to the God who is still at work in the world.

Chapter 9

Navigating Controversy and Division

Every leader, particularly one at the helm of a centuries-old institution like the Church of England, must eventually face the sharp edges of controversy. For Sarah Mullally, controversy was not an unfortunate detour in her ministry but rather a terrain she has had to map, navigate, and at times reimagine. As the first female Bishop of London, her leadership emerged at the crossroads of shifting theology, social reform, and cultural dialogue. This chapter examines four of the most significant and testing areas of division that shaped her ministry and public identity: gender equality in the priesthood, the Church's ongoing conversations about LGBTQ+ inclusion, the difficult task of reconciling tradition with modern realities, and the art of leadership in times of conflict.

Her approach in these areas reveals a delicate balance—pastoral sensitivity intertwined with theological conviction, careful listening matched with quiet but firm decision-making. To understand how she has guided the Church of England through these debates, we must first appreciate the gravity of the issues themselves.

9.1 Gender Equality and the Priesthood Debate

The question of women in leadership has haunted the Church of England for decades, sparking passionate debate both within the clergy and among laity. Sarah Mullally's own appointment as Bishop of London in 2018 placed her at the very heart of this conversation, symbolizing a watershed moment. The office she assumed was not just any diocesan seat but the third most senior position in the Church of England, traditionally seen as the "bishopric of bishops." That it was now occupied by a woman was a statement heard far beyond church walls.

The Historical Context

For centuries, priesthood within the Church of England had been reserved exclusively for men, grounded in interpretations of scripture and tradition that many argued excluded women from sacramental leadership. The debates reached fever pitch during the late 20th century, with the ordination of women as priests first approved in 1992, followed by the consecration of female bishops in 2014.

When the Synod finally voted to allow women bishops, the Church of England attempted to strike a balance: opening doors for women while making provisions for those who, on theological grounds, could not accept their ministry. This compromise created a patchwork of acceptance and resistance within the Church, leaving leaders like Sarah Mullally to embody both the promise and the tension of this new era.

Mullally as a Symbol and a Target

Her appointment was celebrated by many as a victory for gender equality. Supporters hailed her not only as a competent leader but also as a visible example that the Church was moving into a more inclusive future. For young women considering ordination, Mullally's rise sent a powerful signal: the highest offices of the Church were no longer closed to them.

Yet celebration was far from universal. Some saw her appointment as a betrayal of tradition, evidence of the Church yielding to cultural pressure rather than remaining steadfast in its doctrinal convictions. For certain Anglo-Catholics and conservative evangelicals, the sacramental validity of a female bishop was contested, creating real tension in parishes across the diocese.

Mullally did not dismiss these concerns. Instead, she positioned herself as a bridge-builder, acknowledging the pain and conviction on both sides. Her early public statements reflected this posture: she affirmed the validity and importance of women's leadership while pledging to respect and make space for those who could not, in conscience, accept it. This was not an easy position to hold, but it was emblematic of her leadership style—seeking reconciliation without sacrificing conviction.

Pastoral Approach

One of the hallmarks of her approach was a refusal to polarize. She consistently emphasized that unity could not mean uniformity but must instead be grounded in mutual respect. She encouraged dialogue not as a weapon to win arguments but as a space to foster understanding.

This pastoral style mirrored her earlier career in nursing: just as a nurse listens carefully to the patient before offering treatment, Mullally listened deeply to the voices of the divided Church. She framed disagreements not merely as obstacles but as opportunities for Christians to practice what they preached—grace, humility, and compassion.

Long-Term Impact

The debates over women in ministry are far from resolved, but the fact that Sarah Mullally has not only survived but thrived in her role demonstrates the slow but significant shift in the Church's cultural fabric. The controversies of gender equality, once a battlefield, have become in her leadership an ongoing but manageable dialogue.

9.2 The Church and LGBTQ+ Conversations

If gender equality represented a generational battle within the Church of England, the question of LGBTQ+ inclusion remains one of the most urgent and divisive challenges of Mullally's tenure. Unlike the priesthood debate, which eventually found legislative resolution, questions around sexuality and marriage continue to polarize the Church deeply.

The Broader Cultural Shift

Western society has undergone a profound transformation in its understanding of sexuality and identity. Legal recognition of same-sex relationships, shifts in cultural norms, and the increasing visibility of LGBTQ+ voices have pushed institutions, including the Church, into new territory. Where once silence or condemnation dominated, the demand for inclusion and affirmation now resounds loudly.

For the Church of England, these shifts have created tension between tradition and pastoral care. Official teaching holds that marriage is between one man and one woman, yet many clergy and lay leaders openly affirm and bless same-sex couples. This divergence has created a fault line, with bishops caught in the middle.

Mullally's Position and Challenges

As Bishop of London, Sarah Mullally could not avoid these debates. She inherited a diocese that included parishes passionately advocating for LGBTQ+ inclusion and others staunchly opposed to it. Her task was not only to articulate a position but also to shepherd unity among divided congregations.

Her public stance has been marked by careful nuance. She has affirmed the dignity of LGBTQ+ individuals, condemned homophobia, and emphasized the Church's responsibility to offer welcome and pastoral support to all. At the same time, she has recognized the diversity of theological conviction within the Church, resisting calls to impose a unilateral resolution that might fracture communion.

Pastoral Sensitivity

What distinguished Mullally's approach was her capacity to listen. She engaged directly with LGBTQ+ Christians, hearing stories of pain, rejection, and resilience. These encounters shaped her pastoral sensitivity and reinforced her conviction that the Church must never become a place of exclusion.

At the same time, she sought to honor those whose theological convictions made affirmation difficult. For Mullally, leadership in this space meant creating dialogue rather than division, fostering spaces where painful honesty could coexist with mutual respect.

Public Perception

Her position has sometimes drawn criticism from both sides. Advocates of full inclusion argue that her measured stance lacks urgency, accusing her of timidity in the face of injustice. Traditionalists, on the other hand, warn that her openness risks undermining the Church's biblical teaching. Yet Mullally has remained steadfast in holding the tension, refusing to collapse the conversation into simplistic binaries.

The Larger Struggle

The LGBTQ+ debate within the Church is not merely about policy but about identity, theology, and the very meaning of community. Mullally's leadership underscores the impossibility of quick fixes; instead, she embodies a model of patient engagement, where progress is measured not by sweeping resolutions but by the slow, deliberate work of building relationships across differences.

9.3 Reconciling Tradition with Modern Realities

Perhaps the greatest challenge of leading the Church of England in the 21st century is the task of reconciling tradition with modern realities. This challenge is not limited to gender or sexuality but extends to broader questions: What does it mean to be a national church in a post-Christian society? How can ancient liturgy speak to a digital generation? How does one preserve continuity while embracing change?

The Weight of Tradition

The Church of England carries centuries of liturgy, theology, and cultural influence. Its cathedrals, rituals, and hierarchy are steeped in history. For many, this tradition is not a burden but a treasure—an anchor in a fast-changing world. Yet for others, it risks appearing outdated, irrelevant, or even oppressive.

Mullally, deeply aware of this tension, has consistently articulated the need to honor tradition while allowing it to breathe in new contexts. She has resisted the temptation to abandon the past in pursuit of cultural relevance but equally refused to enshrine tradition as untouchable.

Engaging with Modern Society

Her leadership has emphasized dialogue with contemporary issues: healthcare, inequality, climate change, and the role of faith in a secular democracy. She has argued that the Church must not retreat into nostalgia but must engage the pressing questions of the day with courage and compassion.

For example, her background in nursing equipped her to speak authoritatively on issues of health and wellbeing. During public crises, such as the COVID-19 pandemic, she became a voice of both theological reflection and practical guidance, demonstrating how tradition can inform but not constrain modern leadership.

Liturgical Adaptation

One of the ways Mullally has navigated this reconciliation is through liturgical flexibility. She recognizes that while ancient words carry beauty, they must also speak meaningfully to modern lives. Encouraging creative worship, especially in diverse urban contexts like London, she has promoted a Church that is both rooted and responsive.

Challenges of Secularization

Reconciling tradition with modernity also means facing the reality of secularization. Church attendance has declined, and younger generations often see the Church as irrelevant. Mullally has not shied away from this challenge, instead urging the Church to rethink evangelism—not as a campaign of conversion but as an invitation into community, service, and meaning.

9.4 Leadership in Times of Conflict

Conflict is inevitable in an institution as vast and diverse as the Church of England. The real test of leadership is not whether conflict arises but how it is navigated. Sarah

Mullally's episcopal ministry has been shaped by this reality, demanding resilience, discernment, and humility.

The Nature of Church Conflict

Church conflicts are rarely abstract; they are personal, theological, and often deeply emotional. They touch on identity, belief, and belonging. This makes them harder to resolve than organizational disputes, because they involve not only ideas but also souls.

As Bishop of London, Mullally has faced conflicts on multiple fronts: theological disagreements, parish disputes, and broader societal controversies. In each case, she has sought to lead with integrity rather than expediency.

Conflict Resolution Strategies

Her approach to conflict reflects her nursing background once again. Nurses are trained to assess crises calmly, gather information, and act with both compassion and clarity. Mullally brought these instincts into church leadership. She prioritized listening before speaking, understanding before prescribing, and reconciliation before judgment.

She has convened dialogues, facilitated mediation, and encouraged honesty even when it exposed painful truths. Importantly, she has resisted the temptation to silence conflict, instead allowing it to be named and addressed in constructive ways.

Personal Qualities in Leadership

Mullally's calm demeanor and refusal to be drawn into polemics have often defused tensions. Colleagues describe her as steady, thoughtful, and measured—qualities that, in times of heightened conflict, become invaluable. Her style is not authoritarian but collaborative, seeking consensus without abdicating responsibility.

Leading Through Crisis

Her tenure coincided with moments of national and ecclesial crisis: Brexit, the COVID-19 pandemic, and escalating debates over identity and inclusion. In these times, she provided not only organizational leadership but also spiritual guidance. Her sermons and public addresses often emphasized hope, resilience, and the enduring presence of God amid uncertainty.

The Deeper Lesson

Perhaps the deepest lesson of her leadership in conflict is that peace is not the absence of disagreement but the presence of grace. Mullally has modeled a way of leading that does not eliminate division but refuses to let division destroy community.

Holding the Tension

Sarah Mullally's journey through controversy and division reveals a leader unwilling to choose easy answers. Whether in debates over gender, sexuality, tradition, or conflict, she has embraced the complexity of her role. Her legacy in these areas may not be defined by decisive resolutions but by the integrity with which she has held tension, nurtured dialogue, and insisted on compassion.

The Church of England remains a community marked by disagreement. But under her leadership, it has also been reminded that unity does not require uniformity, and that controversy, when navigated with grace, can become a crucible for deeper faith and renewed hope.

Chapter 10

Personal Life, Strengths, and Inspirations

When people think of Sarah Mullally, they often picture her in the public sphere: in her bishop's robes at St Paul's Cathedral, addressing clergy and laity, or being interviewed by journalists about her groundbreaking role as the first female Bishop of London. Yet behind the public image lies a deeply personal story. Her private life, her faith practices, her personal resilience, and the inspirations that shaped her all provide the foundation for her leadership. Understanding Sarah Mullally requires not only studying her public achievements but also exploring the rhythms, disciplines, and values that sustain her as a human being.

This chapter pulls back the curtain on her personal world — her family life, her quiet practices of faith, the ways she has confronted challenges, the mentors who guided her, and the deeply human qualities that make her more than just a historic figure.

10.1 Family and Private Faith Practices

A Life Rooted in Family

Family has always been a vital source of stability and meaning for Sarah Mullally. Unlike many public leaders who allow their work to eclipse their home life, she has consistently emphasized that her identity is not solely defined by her title or position. At home, she is Sarah — not "Bishop Mullally." This distinction is not just symbolic; it reflects her belief that faith and leadership lose authenticity if they are detached from the daily realities of personal relationships.

She is married to Eamonn Mullally, and together they have navigated the often demanding balance between family responsibilities and high-profile public service. Their partnership has been a grounding force in her life, providing companionship and continuity through the unpredictable transitions of career and calling. The Mullally household has never been a stage for public performance; rather, it has been a private sanctuary where faith, conversation, and mutual support flourish.

Her children, too, have been central to her personal life. Parenting, in her view, is both a responsibility and a privilege. Just as in her nursing days she emphasized holistic care — treating patients as whole people, not just conditions — so in family life she sought to nurture her children's emotional, intellectual, and spiritual growth. Even in her busiest years, she carved out time for family meals, shared prayers, and open conversations. Those who know her closely describe her as someone who listens deeply, not only in the professional realm but also at home.

A Faith Practiced Quietly

Despite her prominence, Mullally's private faith practices are intentionally understated. She does not see personal piety as something to be showcased but rather as the quiet engine that powers her life. Prayer, scripture reading, and silence are not optional extras for her; they are the soil from which her resilience grows.

She has often spoken about the importance of silence in a world of noise. For her, silence is not emptiness but presence — a sacred space where she can hear God's voice and regain perspective. She integrates prayer into the ordinary moments of life, whether in the stillness of early morning or in reflective pauses during the day. This rhythm of prayer grounds her decisions and provides clarity in times of uncertainty.

Her faith practices also include communal dimensions. She values the power of worship in community, where individual voices join to create something larger than themselves. Even when serving in high-profile roles, she seeks out opportunities to participate in worship not as a leader but as a member of the congregation, finding strength in shared hymns, sacraments, and prayer.

Holding Tension with Grace

One of the distinctive features of her private faith is her ability to hold tension. As Bishop of London, she deals with communities that represent diverse and sometimes conflicting theological perspectives. In her personal faith, she does not seek to resolve all tensions but to live with them in a spirit of trust. This capacity to accept ambiguity while remaining deeply committed to God's guidance is part of what makes her personal spirituality both realistic and resilient.

Her family and her private practices of faith together form the backbone of her inner life. They provide her with roots deep enough to withstand the storms of controversy, criticism, and leadership challenges. Without these anchors, her public leadership would be unsustainable.

10.2 Personal Resilience and Overcoming Challenges

A Career of Transitions

Resilience is not an abstract virtue for Sarah Mullally; it is a lived reality. From the outside, her career might look like a seamless ascent from nursing to becoming one of the most senior figures in the Church of England. But in reality, her journey was marked by moments of doubt, resistance, and transition.

The move from healthcare to ordained ministry was particularly challenging. She had reached the pinnacle of nursing as England's Chief Nursing Officer, a position that carried immense responsibility and influence.

Walking away from that role was not a step backward but a leap of faith. Many questioned her decision; some could not understand why she would exchange a secure and prestigious career for the uncertainty of ministry. But for Mullally, resilience meant the courage to follow conviction even when others doubted her choices.

Facing Public Scrutiny

Her appointment as Bishop of London was a watershed moment in church history — and with it came public scrutiny on an unprecedented scale. Every statement she made, every decision she took, was analyzed, praised, or criticized by thousands. For some, her gender was still a stumbling block, and her leadership was subjected to skepticism that her male counterparts might not have faced to the same degree.

Yet she approached criticism not with defensiveness but with steadiness. Resilience for her did not mean pretending not to feel the weight of critique; it meant acknowledging it without being crushed by it. She learned to distinguish between constructive criticism that could sharpen her leadership and destructive criticism that had to be set aside.

Physical and Emotional Resilience

Resilience is not only about public leadership; it is also about sustaining one's physical and emotional health. Mullally has long been an advocate of holistic well-being, shaped by her background in nursing. She recognizes that leadership can exact a toll on the body and spirit if not balanced with intentional rest and care.

She prioritizes time for exercise, healthy routines, and rest. More importantly, she practices emotional honesty. Rather than burying stress, she acknowledges it, shares it with trusted confidants, and seeks strength in prayer. This balance allows her to continue leading with clarity rather than exhaustion.

The Power of Saying No

Another aspect of her resilience is the power of boundaries. In high-demand roles, the temptation to say "yes" to every request can be overwhelming. Yet Mullally understands that saying "no" is sometimes the most faithful response. By setting boundaries, she ensures that her leadership remains sustainable over the long haul.

10.3 Inspirations, Mentors, and Spiritual Guides

Family as Inspiration

Much of Sarah Mullally's inspiration flows from her family. Her parents instilled in her the values of service, humility, and perseverance. Their example shaped her vision of leadership not as dominance but as service. She often reflects on the quiet strength of those who influenced her early years — people who may not have held public roles but who modeled integrity and care in daily life.

Mentors in Nursing

Her years in nursing provided her with mentors who demonstrated resilience under pressure. Senior nurses and healthcare leaders showed her what it meant to combine compassion with competence. They taught her that leadership in healthcare is not about power but about service to patients, staff, and the wider community. These lessons stayed with her as she transitioned to church leadership, where the principles of care and service remain central.

Spiritual Guides in Ministry

In ministry, Mullally sought guidance from experienced clergy and theologians who helped her navigate the challenges of ordination and pastoral leadership. These mentors encouraged her to find her own voice rather than merely imitate others. Their wisdom helped her discern her calling more clearly and strengthened her confidence in times of uncertainty.

Historical and Contemporary Inspirations

Beyond personal mentors, Mullally draws inspiration from figures in Christian history. Leaders such as Florence Nightingale, who combined faith with service in healthcare, and pioneering women in ministry who challenged barriers, serve as models for her own path. She also finds inspiration in contemporary voices — theologians, activists, and leaders who embody faith in action.

Her inspirations are not limited to religious figures. Artists, writers, and community leaders who articulate truth with courage also shape her imagination. She values the power of stories, whether from scripture, literature, or lived experience, to inspire resilience and creativity.

10.4 The Human Side of a Public Leader

Grounded in Everyday Life

It is easy to see public leaders as distant or untouchable. Yet those who know Sarah Mullally personally emphasize her warmth, humor, and groundedness. She enjoys ordinary conversations, shares laughter freely, and never allows titles to create barriers. This human side makes her approachable, not only to colleagues but to ordinary parishioners who find in her a leader who listens and understands.

Balancing Public and Private Roles

Her life requires constant negotiation between public duty and private identity. She must represent the Church of England in matters of national importance, yet she also treasures time spent with her family, friends, and community. She manages this balance by keeping her priorities clear: her faith and her family are non-negotiable foundations, and her public role flows from those commitments rather than overshadowing them.

Empathy as Leadership

At the heart of her human side is empathy. She listens not just to respond but to understand. Whether sitting with grieving families, addressing clergy in conflict, or conversing with children in church, she brings a presence that communicates genuine care. This empathy is not a weakness but a strength; it allows her to connect across divides and to lead with authenticity.

Vulnerability and Strength

Her humanity is also revealed in her willingness to acknowledge vulnerability. She does not claim to have all the answers, nor does she hide the struggles of leadership. Instead, she models a kind of strength that embraces vulnerability. In doing so, she offers others permission to be honest about their own struggles, creating communities where authenticity is valued over perfection.

A Life Rooted in Humanity and Faith

The personal life of Sarah Mullally reveals dimensions that cannot be captured by titles alone. Family, private faith practices, resilience, mentors, inspirations, and the very human qualities that shape her interactions — all these elements form the hidden architecture of her public leadership.

Her story reminds us that great leaders are not forged in the spotlight alone. They are shaped in the quiet spaces of prayer, in the resilience born of setbacks, in the wisdom drawn from mentors, and in the laughter and love of family.

For Sarah Mullally, the personal and the public are inseparable. Her leadership flows not from ambition but from authenticity, not from self-promotion but from service. This integration of personal strength and public responsibility is what makes her not only a historic figure in the Church of England but also a leader whose story resonates far beyond ecclesiastical circles.

Chapter 11

Public Speaking, Writings, and Influence

When we trace the arc of Sarah Mullally's life and career, one of the most striking qualities that emerges is her ability to communicate. She has consistently demonstrated that leadership in the twenty-first century is not only about holding a position of authority but also about shaping conversations, bridging divides, and offering hope in a fractured world. Her words—whether delivered from the pulpit, in written form, or through media appearances—carry a weight that transcends her office. They resonate because they come from a place of authenticity, experience, and moral courage.

Mullally's influence cannot be reduced to her historic role as the first female Bishop of London; rather, it extends into the realm of how she speaks, writes, and engages with the public. At the heart of her communication lies a deep conviction that faith must remain relevant, accessible, and transformative. This chapter explores the ways in which she has achieved that through her sermons, publications, theological reflections, and her public presence in broader society.

11.1 Key Sermons and Speeches

For Sarah Mullally, preaching is not an academic exercise nor a platform for showcasing theological prowess; it is a lived dialogue between faith and the pressing realities of the modern world. Her sermons consistently reflect a balance of clarity, compassion, and conviction. They avoid abstraction, instead anchoring theological truths in practical, everyday experiences. This ability to connect across boundaries is what has made her sermons widely recognized not only within the Church of England but also among those outside it.

The Language of Inclusion and Compassion

From her earliest homilies, Mullally emphasized that the Gospel speaks to all, without exception. She has often returned to themes of inclusion, equality, and the inherent dignity of every human being. In major cathedral sermons, she has addressed sensitive issues such as gender inequality, mental health, social justice, and the role of the Church in addressing poverty.

Her words are striking because they combine pastoral gentleness with prophetic urgency. She does not shy away from difficult questions. Instead, she confronts them head-on, weaving scripture with lived experience. This has given her sermons a quality of relevance that many congregants have described as deeply personal and transformative.

Sermons on National Occasions

As Bishop of London, Mullally has had the responsibility of speaking at events of national significance. Whether at St Paul's Cathedral during state commemorations, or at services marking public tragedies, she has been called upon to articulate collective grief and collective hope. In these moments, she has demonstrated an extraordinary gift for empathy.

Her sermon following the Grenfell Tower fire is one such example. Rather than offering platitudes, she chose to acknowledge the raw pain of loss while calling for justice, accountability, and compassion. She did not merely comfort; she challenged both the Church and wider society to ensure such tragedies are not repeated. In doing so, she modeled what it means to speak truth to power while standing alongside the suffering.

Themes of Hope and Renewal

Another recurring aspect of Mullally's sermons is her insistence on hope, even in the bleakest of contexts. Whether addressing congregations in times of political uncertainty, economic hardship, or during the global pandemic, her words have consistently pointed to resilience, faith, and renewal. Hope, for Mullally, is not a passive feeling but an active force—something that calls communities to action.

Her homilies frequently encourage listeners to see themselves as agents of God's healing in the world. This approach has been particularly powerful for younger audiences, who often seek practical relevance in spiritual messages.

Style and Delivery

In terms of delivery, Mullally has a calm but authoritative presence. She does not employ theatrics or emotional manipulation. Instead, she speaks with clarity, carefully measured cadence, and a sense of conviction that draws listeners in. Her background as a nurse—accustomed to both explaining complex issues simply and speaking with compassion—has shaped her communication style. Listeners often remark that she speaks as though addressing each person individually, even in vast cathedrals filled with thousands.

Through these key sermons and speeches, Mullally has become not only a leader of the Church but also a moral voice for the nation—someone capable of interpreting both scripture and society in ways that illuminate paths forward.

11.2 Published Works and Contributions to Theology

Sarah Mullally's written contributions, though not as prolific as career academics, reflect the same qualities as her spoken words: accessibility, relevance, and depth. She writes not for ivory-tower theologians alone but for lay readers, parish leaders, and those grappling with faith in daily life. Her works blend theological reflection with pastoral insight, making them valuable resources for individuals and communities seeking guidance.

Articles and Essays

Throughout her ministry, Mullally has contributed to journals, magazines, and Church of England publications. Her essays often focus on themes of health, healing, and the integration of faith with professional life. Given her background in nursing, she has offered unique perspectives on the intersections of physical, emotional, and spiritual well-being.

Her writings also engage with contemporary debates in the Church, particularly around inclusion, gender equality, and the role of the Church in addressing social injustice. While she does not write polemics, her essays display courage in naming uncomfortable truths and calling the Church to greater faithfulness.

Books and Theological Reflections

Though she is not primarily known as a prolific author of theological books, Mullally's contributions often come in the form of chapters within edited collections, official Church reports, and collaborative theological projects. In these, her emphasis is consistently on praxis—the lived application of theology. She resists overly academic jargon, preferring instead to show how theology matters in the wards of hospitals, the streets of London, or the homes of ordinary families.

Her reflections often circle around the theme of vocation. For her, vocation is not limited to clergy or religious leaders but encompasses the calling of all Christians to live faithfully in their respective fields—whether medicine, teaching, business, or domestic life. This democratization of vocation reflects her conviction that the Church is strongest when all its members recognize their role in God's mission.

Theology of Care and Healing

A distinctive contribution of Mullally's writings lies in her theology of care. She brings together the worlds of healthcare and Christian faith in ways that enrich both. Her perspective suggests that healing is not only about curing illness but about restoring dignity, addressing loneliness, and affirming the worth of every individual.

She has written persuasively about the Church's responsibility to embody this healing in society. For Mullally, churches are not simply places of worship but also places of refuge, belonging, and holistic support. This approach has influenced both parish-level ministry and broader theological conversations about the Church's role in public life.

The Pastoral Voice in Writing

Readers often note that her writing carries the same pastoral tone as her sermons. Even when addressing complex theological issues, she writes with an accessibility that feels like a conversation rather than a lecture. This quality has made her works appealing not only to scholars but also to parishioners and those exploring faith.

In sum, her contributions to theology—though not measured by volume—are measured by depth and practical significance. She has carved a space where theology is not an abstract discipline but a lived, breathing reality that speaks to modern concerns.

11.3 Influence Beyond the Pulpit

Sarah Mullally's influence is far from confined to church buildings. She has consistently emphasized that the Church must be engaged with society in tangible ways, and she has modeled this herself. Her leadership, public statements, and initiatives have reached into spheres such as healthcare, education, politics, and community development.

Health and Well-Being

Given her background as Chief Nursing Officer for England, Mullally has remained deeply involved in conversations around health and well-being. She often bridges the gap between faith and medicine, showing that the two need not be at odds. Her advocacy for mental health awareness, palliative care, and holistic approaches to wellness has made her a trusted voice in both ecclesial and healthcare circles.

In speeches and writings, she frequently reminds audiences that healthcare is not only about efficiency and outcomes but about compassion, justice, and the recognition of human dignity. Her dual expertise allows her to speak to healthcare professionals with authority while also challenging the Church to become a more healing presence.

Social Justice and Public Life

Mullally has also taken strong positions on issues of social justice. From poverty and inequality to racism and gender-based violence, she consistently calls for the Church to be on the side of the marginalized. Her influence beyond the pulpit often takes the form of advocacy—speaking at conferences, contributing to public debates, or supporting community initiatives that address systemic injustice.

Her leadership during the COVID-19 pandemic demonstrated this influence vividly. She was vocal about the need to balance restrictions with compassion, to support frontline workers, and to ensure that vulnerable communities were not left behind. In doing so, she became a voice of both caution and encouragement in a time of global crisis.

Mentorship and Inspiration

Another way Mullally exerts influence beyond the pulpit is through her role as a mentor and role model. For countless women considering ordination or leadership in the Church, her journey stands as living proof that barriers can be broken. She has taken time to encourage younger clergy, often reminding them that leadership is not about power but about service.

Her ability to inspire extends beyond the clergy. Many lay Christians, particularly those in healthcare, education, and social work, have found in her story a model for integrating faith with professional life. She embodies the conviction that service in secular arenas can be just as sacred as service within the Church.

Engaging Wider Society

Perhaps most importantly, Mullally has succeeded in engaging people outside the traditional boundaries of the Church. She frequently participates in interfaith dialogues, cultural events, and civic ceremonies. In doing so, she presents Christianity not as an isolated institution but as a faith that speaks to the shared challenges of humanity.

Her influence, therefore, is not limited to those who sit in pews on Sunday mornings. It extends to hospital wards, parliamentary debates, university halls, and community centers—wherever conversations about meaning, justice, and compassion are taking place.

11.4 Presence in Media and Public Discourse

In the twenty-first century, leaders cannot ignore the power of the media. Sarah Mullally has embraced this reality with wisdom and discernment. While she has not sought celebrity status, she has understood that media engagement is part of her responsibility as a public figure.

A Measured Media Presence

Unlike some public leaders who court controversy for attention, Mullally's media strategy has been measured. She appears in interviews, documentaries, and news coverage primarily to address issues of significance— whether a theological debate within the Church, a national tragedy, or a public health matter.

Her media presence is characterized by clarity and calmness. She avoids sensationalism, choosing instead to communicate in ways that invite reflection rather than provoke division. This has earned her respect across political and social divides.

Speaking to a Secular Audience

One of her most notable strengths in media appearances is her ability to speak to secular audiences without diluting her faith. She communicates the heart of Christian teaching in language that resonates with those who may not share her beliefs. This is a rare skill and one that has allowed her to extend the Church's relevance beyond traditional boundaries.

For example, in interviews on issues such as mental health or inequality, she frames her arguments in universal values—dignity, justice, compassion—while remaining clear about the Christian foundations of her convictions. This balance has made her a trusted voice in conversations that often exclude religious perspectives.

Navigating Controversy

Inevitably, as a high-profile leader, Mullally has faced media scrutiny. On divisive issues—such as the role of women in the Church or debates around sexuality—she has been careful yet firm. She refuses to reduce complex matters to soundbites, insisting on nuance and pastoral sensitivity. While this sometimes frustrates critics seeking clear-cut answers, it reflects her belief that faith requires discernment and dialogue rather than simplistic slogans.

Her ability to remain gracious under pressure has enhanced her credibility. Even when facing hostile questions, she maintains composure and returns to core principles of compassion and integrity.

Influence Through Visibility

Finally, her presence in the media contributes to a broader cultural visibility of women in leadership within the Church. Simply by appearing in these spaces—as the Bishop of London, dressed in clerical robes, articulating complex issues—she challenges stereotypes and expands public imagination of who can lead. This visibility is itself a form of influence, shaping perceptions for future generations.

Sarah Mullally's legacy is inseparable from her ability to communicate. Whether in the pulpit, on the page, in the corridors of power, or on television screens, she speaks with a voice that blends compassion with courage. Her sermons provide clarity in times of confusion. Her writings bring theology into conversation with everyday life. Her influence extends far beyond the Church, shaping debates on health, justice, and inclusion. And her presence in the media demonstrates that faith, when expressed authentically, still has a vital place in public discourse.

Ultimately, Mullally exemplifies the truth that words, when rooted in conviction and compassion, can change hearts, shape institutions, and inspire societies. Her story reminds us that leadership is not only about what one does but also about how one communicates—and in this, she stands as one of the most compelling voices of her generation.

Chapter 12

Legacy in the Making

Legacy is not only what we leave behind but what we inspire in the present, what we kindle in others, and how our choices ripple through generations. For Sarah Mullally, the question of legacy cannot be confined to a list of achievements, titles, or positions. Instead, it must be understood as an unfolding story that continues to evolve. She embodies a legacy of faith rooted in courage, compassion, and conviction, but she also represents something far more profound: the breaking of barriers in both healthcare and the Church of England, the living out of Christian service in the twenty-first century, and the reshaping of how leadership—especially female leadership—is perceived in modern Christianity.

This chapter explores Sarah Mullally's legacy in four dimensions: what she represents in modern Christianity, how she inspires future generations of women leaders, her enduring impact on healthcare and faith, and the idea of a living legacy—one that continues to be written in real time.

12.1 What Sarah Mullally Represents in Modern Christianity

To understand Sarah Mullally's representation in modern Christianity, one must first consider the state of the Church of England and global Christianity in the early twenty-first century. Christianity, particularly in Western societies, finds itself at a crossroads: grappling with declining attendance, cultural skepticism, and the need to reconcile long-held traditions with rapidly shifting societal values. In this landscape, Mullally represents a bridge between tradition and transformation, embodying both continuity with the Church's heritage and an openness to new expressions of faith and service.

At the heart of her legacy is the role she played in normalizing female leadership within the Church. The Church of England's decision to allow women bishops in 2014 was itself a monumental shift after centuries of male-only episcopal leadership. Just four years later, in 2018, Sarah Mullally became the Bishop of London—the third most senior position in the Church of England, surpassed only by the Archbishop of Canterbury and the Archbishop of York. Her appointment was historic not merely for its symbolism but for its practical demonstration that women could assume leadership of one of the most visible dioceses in the Anglican Communion.

Her rise to prominence also reframed debates about what leadership in the Church could look like. Instead of adopting the traditionally hierarchical and authoritative model of leadership, she brought a servant-leadership approach shaped by her background in healthcare. This emphasis on care, listening, and collaboration resonated with many who had grown disillusioned by rigid clerical structures. In her leadership style, Mullally represents a vision of Christianity that is both pastoral and prophetic—tender in care yet bold in vision.

Another critical aspect of what she represents is the integration of professional expertise and faith. Few leaders of her stature can claim to have reached the heights of two distinct professions. Her career as Chief Nursing Officer for England demonstrated not only her competence in healthcare leadership but also her dedication to serving the public good. By transitioning into ordained ministry and episcopal leadership, she modeled the idea that secular and sacred vocations are not opposed but deeply intertwined. She shows modern Christianity that faith need not be siloed away from professional life; rather, it can infuse and shape every sphere of influence.

Mullally also represents resilience in the face of division. The Church of England, like many Christian denominations, is marked by debates over gender, sexuality, and the interpretation of Scripture. In these contested spaces, her leadership has been one of patient listening and bridge-building. Though criticized at times from both conservative and progressive camps, she has insisted that her role is not to take sides but to create spaces for dialogue, mutual respect, and discernment. In this way, she represents a model of leadership that prioritizes unity without erasing difference.

Lastly, she embodies the possibility of a Christianity that is relevant to modern life. Her work consistently seeks to engage with issues such as healthcare equity, social justice, and public health, showing that Christian faith is not only about personal piety but about collective well-being. In her, modern Christianity finds a leader who can speak credibly to both the Church and the wider world.

In sum, Sarah Mullally represents:

A breaking of barriers for women in ecclesiastical leadership.

A servant-leadership model rooted in healthcare and compassion.

The integration of faith and professional excellence.

A reconciling presence in a divided Church.

A vision of Christianity that speaks to modern challenges.

12.2 Inspiring Future Generations of Women Leaders

Perhaps the most enduring aspect of Mullally's legacy will be her role in inspiring and empowering future generations of women leaders. Leadership in the Church has long been marked by male dominance, and women's voices were historically marginalized or confined to certain roles. By stepping into the episcopacy, and later the bishopric of London, Mullally shattered centuries of precedent and opened doors for countless women who might otherwise have doubted whether they belonged at the highest levels of ecclesiastical leadership.

Her story offers a powerful narrative of possibility. For women discerning their vocations, her journey demonstrates that barriers—though daunting—are not immovable. She shows that leadership is not defined by gender but by calling, gifting, and faithfulness. When young women see her presiding over liturgies at St. Paul's Cathedral, speaking to Parliament, or engaging with healthcare leaders, they see tangible proof that women can lead, influence, and transform the Church and society alike.

But her inspiration goes deeper than visibility. Sarah Mullally has consistently emphasized mentorship, encouragement, and the cultivation of others' gifts. By modeling a collaborative style of leadership, she has demonstrated that women in positions of authority need not replicate patriarchal or authoritarian patterns but can lead in ways that affirm, empower, and build up others. This alternative model of leadership is itself transformative, offering a new paradigm for what it means to hold power responsibly.

For women outside the Church, particularly in healthcare and public service, her legacy also resonates. Her dual careers showcase the possibility of integrating multiple vocations and refusing to be limited by traditional boundaries. To young women in medicine, nursing, or public policy, her life stands as a reminder that faith and professional excellence can coexist, and that women need not choose between one or the other.

Her legacy also extends into education and public imagination. Schools, universities, and theological colleges increasingly highlight her journey as an example of resilience, calling, and courage. She represents not just the first woman Bishop of London but also a woman who rose to senior leadership without abandoning her authenticity, compassion, or humility.

For the Church of England, her example sets a precedent that cannot be undone. Now that women have occupied some of the highest offices, future generations will grow up in a Church where female leadership is normalized rather than exceptional. Her role thus marks a turning point in the story of Anglican leadership, ensuring that the next generation will see leadership not through the lens of exclusion but of shared calling.

In short, Sarah Mullally inspires women leaders by:

Providing visibility in positions historically denied to women.

Modeling an alternative, collaborative leadership style.

Encouraging integration of faith with professional excellence.

Serving as an educational and cultural role model.

Normalizing women's leadership for future generations of Anglicans.

12.3 Her Enduring Impact on Healthcare and Faith

Sarah Mullally's legacy cannot be fully appreciated without acknowledging her profound contributions to both healthcare and faith. These two worlds, often perceived as separate, intersect in her life in a way that enriches both and offers a holistic model of leadership.

Her healthcare career is extraordinary in its own right. As England's Chief Nursing Officer, she oversaw the nation's nursing workforce, advocated for patient-centered care, and guided policy decisions that affected millions. She brought to that role not only technical expertise but also a deep empathy for patients and families. Her tenure coincided with significant challenges in the National Health Service, and she navigated those challenges with pragmatism, resilience, and an unwavering commitment to public service.

The transition from healthcare to ordained ministry could have been perceived as a sharp break. Instead, Mullally carried the values of nursing—compassion, service, and advocacy—into her ministry. In doing so, she reminded both the Church and society that caring for bodies and caring for souls are not separate tasks but interconnected dimensions of human flourishing. Her work shows that faith is not abstract but profoundly embodied, concerned with the real conditions of life, suffering, and healing.

In her episcopal leadership, she has consistently addressed issues of public health, inequality, and justice. During the COVID-19 pandemic, for instance, her dual background positioned her uniquely to speak credibly on matters of faith and science. She was able to encourage adherence to public health measures while also providing pastoral care to those grieving, isolated, or overwhelmed by fear. In this moment, her legacy of integrating healthcare and faith was vividly displayed.

Her advocacy has also extended to mental health, poverty alleviation, and the social determinants of health. She has articulated a vision in which the Church is not merely a spiritual refuge but an active agent of social transformation. In this sense, her impact resonates far beyond ecclesiastical circles and touches the lives of countless people who may never step foot inside a cathedral.

Theologically, her healthcare background has enriched her understanding of ministry. Nursing taught her the value of presence—of being with others in moments of vulnerability. This attentiveness has become a hallmark of her pastoral ministry. It has also shaped her preaching, where she often draws connections between faith and lived human experience.

Her enduring impact, then, lies in her demonstration that healthcare and faith are not rivals but partners. The healing of bodies and the healing of souls are part of the same vocation of service. By embodying both, she has left a model that future leaders—whether in healthcare, ministry, or both—can aspire to emulate.

12.4 A Living Legacy – Still Writing Her Story

Perhaps the most compelling aspect of Sarah Mullally's legacy is that it remains unfinished. Unlike many figures whose legacies are assessed only after their deaths, Mullally's is a living legacy—one that continues to unfold, adapt, and inspire in real time.

Her story resists easy closure because she remains active at the center of both ecclesiastical and societal life. Every sermon she preaches, every decision she makes, and every initiative she leads contributes to the ongoing narrative of her influence. This means her legacy is dynamic rather than static, and it invites us not only to reflect on what she has achieved but also to anticipate what she will yet do.

The concept of a living legacy is particularly fitting for a Christian leader, as it underscores the idea that faith is never finished but always unfolding. Mullally herself often emphasizes the importance of journey, growth, and transformation. Her life reflects this theology: she has continually embraced new callings, transitioned between vocations, and adapted to the evolving needs of the Church and society.

This living legacy also means that her impact cannot be confined to one generation. By mentoring younger leaders, advocating for systemic change, and speaking to contemporary issues, she ensures that her influence will ripple outward long after her tenure as Bishop of London. Her work plants seeds whose fruits may not be visible for decades, but which will nonetheless shape the future of the Church and public life.

Her ongoing story also raises questions about the future of the Church of England itself. As debates continue over doctrine, inclusion, and mission, Mullally remains a central voice helping to navigate these challenges. Her living legacy includes the ongoing task of shaping how the Church will adapt to twenty-first-century realities while remaining faithful to its core convictions.

Finally, her living legacy challenges us as readers to consider our own. By refusing to see her life as complete, she reminds us that legacy is not something reserved for those who have finished their course. It is something we all create daily, through our choices, values, and actions. Mullally invites us into that same reflection: what will our own legacy be, and how will we live in such a way that others are uplifted, inspired, and transformed?

Sarah Mullally's legacy is multifaceted, stretching across healthcare, faith, leadership, and cultural transformation. She represents the breaking of barriers in modern Christianity, inspires future generations of women leaders, integrates the worlds of healthcare and faith, and continues to live out a legacy that is still being written. Her life is not merely a story of personal achievement but a testimony to what it means to live faithfully, courageously, and compassionately in a world that hungers for hope and integrity.

Her legacy, in the end, is not just hers. It belongs to those she has healed, taught, mentored, and inspired. It belongs to the Church of England, now forever changed by her leadership. It belongs to the healthcare professionals who see in her life the sacredness of their vocation. And it belongs to all of us who, through her story, are reminded that legacies are not monuments to the past but seeds for the future.

Conclusion

Reflections on Leadership, Faith, and Service

As we reach the close of Sarah Mullally's remarkable journey so far, it is impossible to treat her life story as finished. The truth is that her journey is still unfolding, still challenging the assumptions of both Church and society, and still inspiring those who search for examples of courageous, compassionate, and visionary leadership. Yet, it is precisely at this point—standing at the edge of what has been and what is yet to come—that reflection becomes most valuable.

Sarah Mullally's story is not only that of an individual rising through the ranks of nursing, theology, and ecclesiastical office. It is also the story of a nation grappling with questions of faith in a rapidly changing cultural landscape. It is the story of a Church wrestling with its history, its traditions, and its future. And it is the story of a woman who has consistently put service before status, calling before comfort, and conviction before compromise.

To reflect on her leadership is to encounter a model shaped by dual vocations: one rooted in the practical, urgent realities of healthcare, and another rooted in the spiritual, eternal dimensions of faith. Nursing taught her attentiveness, empathy, and the ability to make decisions under pressure. The ministry demanded the same qualities, but reframed them in the context of souls rather than bodies, communities rather than wards, eternal truths rather than temporary crises. Together, these dual threads of service formed the tapestry of her leadership style—a leadership not driven by power or prestige, but by presence, compassion, and courage.

Her life reminds us that true leadership is not about commanding others from a distance but about walking alongside them, listening to their struggles, and helping them imagine possibilities they could not see alone. Leadership, for her, has always been less about authority and more about responsibility, less about personal ambition and more about communal flourishing. This emphasis on service-driven leadership is a direct challenge to the models of power that dominate politics, business, and sometimes even religion itself. In Mullally's model, leadership begins and ends with love.

But leadership alone cannot account for the power of her story. At its core, Sarah Mullally's life has been an embodiment of faith—a faith that refuses to stay confined within church walls but spills into hospitals, communities, debates, and daily life. It is a faith that affirms the sacredness of human dignity, insists on justice, and refuses to treat tradition as an immovable stone but rather as a living stream that must continue to flow.

Service, finally, has been the thread holding leadership and faith together. It is service that moved her into nursing, service that drew her into ministry, and service that keeps her grounded as Bishop of London. Service for Sarah Mullally is not abstract or rhetorical; it is embodied, concrete, and demanding. It is found in the exhausted nurse on a night shift, the grieving family in a parish church, the young woman discerning her place in ministry, and the broken city searching for hope. Her service is not glamorous, but it is transformative, precisely because it is grounded in the real.

The reflection, then, is clear: Sarah Mullally's story teaches us that leadership, faith, and service are not separate virtues to be balanced, but interwoven realities to be lived.

The Continuing Journey of Sarah Mullally

When considering the life of someone still very much active in her calling, the temptation is to treat her current status as the pinnacle. After all, the Bishop of London is one of the most historically prestigious and symbolically powerful roles in the Anglican tradition. But for Sarah Mullally, the journey is not about prestige or titles—it is about what comes next.

Her continuing journey is shaped by multiple challenges: the decline of religious participation in the United Kingdom, generational shifts in attitudes toward faith, ongoing debates within the Anglican Communion, and the Church of England's role in a multicultural, multifaith society. Each of these challenges demands wisdom, courage, and imagination.

In some ways, her journey is one of tension. On one hand, she is called to preserve the treasures of tradition, guarding the truths of Scripture and the heritage of the Church. On the other hand, she is compelled to face the pressing questions of today: inclusion, justice, equality, and the credibility of faith in a skeptical age. Walking this tension is not easy. To lean too heavily toward tradition risks alienating those who yearn for progress. To lean too far into change risks losing the anchor of continuity. Mullally's gift has been her ability to inhabit that middle space—not as a compromise, but as a creative space where faith can grow without severing its roots.

The continuing journey is also personal. She remains a wife, a mother, a friend, a mentor, and a woman of prayer. Her leadership is public, but her grounding is deeply private. It is in the rhythms of her own spiritual life, her time in reflection and prayer, her conversations with loved ones, and her attentiveness to God's call that she finds the strength to carry the weight of her role. This duality— public leader and private disciple—remains the heartbeat of her continuing journey.

Looking ahead, one can imagine Sarah Mullally leaving a legacy not just of titles held but of lives touched. Her story will continue to evolve as she responds to crises we cannot yet predict, as she nurtures future leaders who will take the Church further than she could, and as she redefines what it means to live faithfully in a world that is increasingly uncertain.

The journey, in other words, is far from over. It is still being written, and the pages to come may prove just as significant, if not more so, than the pages already turned.

What Readers Can Take from Her Life

The conclusion of a story is never simply about the subject—it is also about the reader. To read the life of Sarah Mullally is not only to learn about her, but to discover truths about ourselves, about leadership, about faith, and about the human capacity for transformation.

The first lesson readers can take is that vocation is rarely linear. Mullally's journey from nursing to the highest levels of the Church defies expectations. It demonstrates that calling is not confined to one profession or one identity, but is dynamic, unfolding, and often surprising. For those who feel locked into a single path, her life is a testimony that new chapters are always possible, and that every experience, no matter how different, can prepare us for the next.

The second lesson is that resilience and courage matter. Whether facing the intensity of healthcare leadership, the skepticism surrounding women in episcopal roles, or the scrutiny of media and public life, Sarah Mullally has shown that true resilience is not about hardness but about persistence rooted in hope. Courage, in her story, does not mean the absence of fear but the decision to act faithfully despite it.

The third lesson is the transformative power of service. In a world often driven by self-interest and ambition, her example reminds us that service to others is not weakness but strength. It is through serving others that one earns trust, credibility, and influence. For readers, whether leaders in business, education, ministry, or family life, this model of service-based leadership is both challenging and liberating.

The fourth lesson is the importance of faith that engages with the real world. Mullally's Christianity is not retreatist or insular. It is outward-looking, engaged, and willing to enter difficult conversations about justice, equality, and inclusion. For those who wonder whether faith can still speak to today's issues, her example shows that it not only can but must.

Finally, the overarching lesson is that legacy is not something to be pursued for its own sake but something that emerges when one lives with integrity, compassion, and conviction. Sarah Mullally is building a legacy not because she sought one, but because she has consistently chosen to serve, to listen, and to lead with courage.

For readers, then, her life is both a mirror and a map. A mirror, because it reflects our own questions, struggles, and hopes. A map, because it points us toward what is possible when service, faith, and courage guide our steps.

The story of Sarah Mullally is not only about a woman who rose to one of the highest offices in the Church of England. It is about the deeper truth that leadership grounded in service can change institutions, communities, and individuals. It is about the possibility that faith, when lived authentically, still has the power to inspire in an age of skepticism. It is about the courage to step into roles no one thought possible and to do so not for personal gain, but for the flourishing of others.

As the final page turns, one cannot help but feel that the real conclusion is not an ending but an invitation. An invitation to take the lessons of Sarah Mullally's story and live them out in our own contexts. To lead with compassion. To serve with humility. To embrace faith not as a retreat from the world but as a force for transformation within it.

In that sense, the story of Sarah Mullally is not hers alone. It is a shared story—a reminder that all of us are called, in our own ways, to lives of leadership, faith, and service.

And perhaps that is the greatest conclusion of all: her life reminds us that we, too, can be part of writing a story worth telling.

Printed in Dunstable, United Kingdom